The Year's Work in Medievalism

Edited by Gwendolyn A. Morgan

XVIV
2004

Wipf & Stock Publishers
Eugene, Oregon

The Year's Work in Medievalism

Series Editor, Gwendolyn Morgan

The Year's Work in Medievalism, volume XIV, is based upon but not restricted to the 2004 proceedings of the Annual International Conference on Medievalism in Fredericton, Canada, organized by the Director of Conferences of *Studies in Medievalism,* and, for 2004, Christa Canitz. *The Year's Work in Medievalism* also publishes bibliographies, book reviews, and announcements of conferences and other events.

The 2004 volume is indexed in *The Modern Language Association International Bibliography.*

Copyright © *Studies in Medievalism* 2006

ISBN 1-59752-781-5

First published in 2006 by Wipf and Stock Publishers
199 West 8th Ave., Suite 3
Eugene, OR 97401
http://www.wipfandstock.com/Publish.htm
for *Studies in Medievalism*

The Year's Work in Medievalism is an imprint of *Studies in Medievalism.* For the series, generally, write Gwendolyn Morgan, Editor, *The Year's Work in Medievalism,* Department of English, Montana State University, Bozeman, MT 59717.

The Year's Work in Medievalism
Volume XVIV 2004

Introduction: Medievalism and Individual Responsibility

Gwendolyn A. Morgan

This issue of *The Year's Work in Medievalism* concentrates on nineteenth- and twentieth-century re-imaginings of the Middle Ages which, as all such practices do, attempt to validate an age's ideas by locating their sources in the medieval past. However, rather than simply present the individual essays in chronological order, or even by genre, I have attempted to juxtapose seemingly unrelated studies to indicate an underlying *sameness* in the medievalistic endeavors that they examine, for all concern themselves with employing the Middle Ages in attempts to increase the humanity of their own. Moreover, the present collection quite neatly illustrates a number of Umberto Eco's "ten little Middle Ages," as detailed in his seminal essay "Dreaming the Middle Ages."[1] Thus, in contrast to Eco's assertions, the various perceptions of the period can and are turned to near identical ends, regardless of whether it is perceived in a positive or negative light.

In Karl Fugelso's discussion of three vastly different interpretations of Dante in nineteenth-century illustrations of his *Divine Comedy*, we see a return to medieval practices on two levels. First, all of the artists discussed return, to a greater or lesser extent, to classical and neoclassical artistic and philosophical principles to validate their visions, recalling the constant appeal to ancient classical authority of the Middle Ages. Of the nineteenth-century artists, most emphatic in doing so is Luigi Ademolli, who not only adheres to ancient principles for sublime style and composition, despite the graphic and often grotesque nature of Dante's text and medieval illustrations of it, but actually ignores the most dramatic and horrific scenes of the poem in order to concentrate on classical subjects for his images. In consequence, he minimizes Dante's incisive examination of the human condition and its attendant spiritual dilemmas, instead favoring a more stylized and distanced reading of the *Comedy*. In other words, his idealized bodies *de*humanize the subjects by their very perfection, and his avoidance of scenes which relate spiritual consequences to human choice removes the reader/viewer from immediate engagement with the text and thereby from participating in its humanity. In contrast, Joseph Anton Koch returns to a specifically medieval style (as powerful a return to ancient practices to validate his vision as Ademolli's appeal to the classical), choice of subject matter, and original illustrations for his work. Although these render *less* visually naturalistic depictions than the classical and neoclassical principles employed by Ademolli, they nonetheless, and paradoxically, render a more emotional connection for the reader/viewer, inviting identification with the characters of Dante's epic and hence engagement with the moral and spiritual questions it raises. In short, it makes the tale more human, and the reaction of the viewer more sympathetic and *humane*.

Interestingly, neoclassical and medieval interpretations of the same subject also inform Renee Ward's reading of Remus Lupin, the werewolf figure in J.K. Rowling's *Harry Potter and the Prisoner and Azkaban*. Lupin is, on the surface, the bestial, vicious abomination of Ovid's (and earlier Greek) myth, deserving of ostracization and destruction, and is treated as such by much of the wizarding community. On the other hand, as Harry and his companions—and by extension, the reader—come to understand, Lupin is one of the most humane characters in the book, a sympathetic outsider made more compassionate in his own views by his very marginalization. This interpretation Ward finds rooted in the medieval tradition of the werewolf, epitomized by Marie's de France's lai "Bisclavret." As with the illustrations examined by Fugelso, the classical tradition serves to dehumanize and distance, to isolate the individual, while the medieval evokes tolerance, understanding, and empathy. Both for certain characters within Rowling's tale and the reader, the double vision of the werewolf Lupin serves to emphasize that humaneness and community are the results of conscious choice. And emerging from both essays is the, perhaps surprising, realization that the medieval view is the more sympathetic of the two offered.

In Nancy Thompson's study of the stained-glass and architectural restoration of Siena's churches during the period following Tuscany's reunification with Italy, we find overt expression of Eco's Middle Ages as Golden Past, put to what is, perhaps, its most common use: a source of national identity and pride. In an effort to remove the "decadent" influence of foreign rule over native culture, the architects and artists of Siena restored numerous churches, returning to the original design and ornamentation of the medieval artists in doing so. Such not only appealed to native spirit and art, but was justified as more spiritual—the Middle Ages were interpreted as a more pious and "pure" era. Both in concert with and in contrast to this effort is the nineteenth-century reinvention of Edward, the Black Prince, as England's national icon, examined by Barbara Gribling. Again driven by the Middle Ages re-imagined as a golden paternal age, in this instance of English nationalism, the elevation of Edward is not, however, for his medieval qualities, which as Gribling demonstrates were more in accordance with transnational class solidarity. Rather, the Black Prince is garbed as the Victorian "gentleman," embracing the humanitarian ideals of an England growing more socially conscious. Hence, a purely contemporary ideal is superimposed on the medieval past to prove contemporary English ideology a cultural and ethnic heritage. Interestingly, Clare Simmons' discussion of *Punch* in the same period, specifically its use of medieval cartoon, ballad, and illumination, depends upon an entirely different conception of the medieval past. *Punch*'s editors and readers apparently subscribe to Eco's "barbaric

Middle Ages" as the premise for using these medieval forms to emphasize the inhumanity of everything from contemporary industrial practices ("Song of the Shirt") to international politics (cartoons depicting politicians as choosing between the poison and dagger offered Fair Rosamund by Queen Eleanor). Apparently, in this case England's medieval heritage lay in the most despicable practices of Victorian England. Nonetheless, no matter how differently *Punch* and the champions of Prince Edward re-imagined the Middle Ages, both employ them to humanize their own era.

In the two essays concerning the fiction of J.R.R. Tolkien, the practice of reviving or adopting what is good in the medieval past to inform and improve the present day (another of Eco's "little Middle Ages") comes to the fore. Brian Johnsrud takes a fresh look at Tolkien's own medievalism and, while recognizing general scholarly consensus that Tolkien attempts to revitalize the "northern theory of courage" and plunders Germanic myth for his own Christian mythos, also sees his rehabilitation of the Nordic pantheon and cauldron of tales not merely as a Christianizing of the mythos but a recognition of purely pagan values. In other words, Middle-earth is not merely a pre-Christian world ready for the advent of Christ, but a pagan world to be valued on its own terms. Similarly, Jaimie Hensley finds another vein to be mined by Tolkien's medievalism, heretofore unacknowledged, in the work of medieval poet Walther von der Volgelweide, which not only provides grist for the creative story-telling process but a realization of "faerie," as imagined by Tolkien, from a patently *non*-Celtic source. Both essays re-examine how Tolkien attempted to work between primary and secondary realities, and both address the spiritual crisis he felt was facing modern man, but both also recognize the value of the purely pagan within the long-recognized Catholic framework of his fiction. Finally, Peter Christensen's analysis of Naomi Mitchison's novel *To the Chapel Perilous* also finds a modern author exploiting medieval myth to demonstrate the need to personalize, humanize, and individualize spirituality. According to Christensen, Mitchison's Grail is necessarily an endless quest and each human being a quester, finding his or her own truth while denying the efficacy of established, common religions. Making the pagan grails more attractive and potent than the Christian is her way of asserting that divine truth is also individual truth found by individual choice, and that such a necessary search is inherent in the human condition.

Thus, in some respects all of the essays in the present collection are concerned with the individual conditions and responsibilities of our existence, and with using the Middle Ages as a way to make contemporary life just a little more humane. Whether the object of militant nostalgia and recreation, condemned as a barbaric age, or adapted to invest moral value into a present, the medieval period remains the source of our spiritual currency. As Eco observes, we return to it as the source of contemporary dilemmas, as our

Gwendolyn A. Morgan

psychic childhood from which we might discover why we are who we are and thereby endeavor to improve ourselves.

MONTANA STATE UNIVERSITY

NOTES

[1] In *Travels in Hyperreality*, trans. William Weaver. NY: Harcourt Brace, 1986.

Defining Medievalism in
Nineteenth-Century *Commedia* Illustrations[1]

Karl Fugelso

In an earlier article, I examined how Henry Fuseli, William Blake, and Gustave Doré responded to Dante's *Divine Comedy* and to pre-modern images of it.[2] In this paper I would like to extend that investigation to a few of their less famous contemporaries, namely Joseph Anton Koch, Luigi Ademolli, and Francesco Scaramuzza.[3] But rather than attempt to discern whether these three illustrators adhered to Neo-Gothic principles of art, much less to Romantic definitions of the sublime, I would like to address whether they were, in fact, even medievalists.

All three depict a text that many of their contemporaries treated as the epitome of medieval literature. Moreover, all three do so in terms that at least somewhat agree with late eighteenth- and nineteenth-century interpretations of medieval art. Yet all three also depend heavily on classical and neo-classical sources, on works that have frequently been considered incompatible with those of the Middle Ages.[4] Thus, all three call into question the purpose and flexibility of medievalism, its ability to tolerate, assimilate, and even build on styles that have often been considered antithetical to it and its sources.

Moreover, all three thereby problematize intentionality. They invite us to ask whether, in fact, they even perceived their allusions as medievalist or neo-classicist, much less deliberately combined them. Could these artists actually have been oblivious to the sources of their references and, by extension, to the supposed incompatibilities among those references? And even if they were aware of those supposed incompatibilities, is it possible that they perceived their allusions as compatible under the circumstances in which they deployed them, that, in the pursuit of a particular effect or group of effects, they felt free to blend medievalism and neo-classicism?

Of course, as is true for many other inquiries pertaining to intentionality, these questions are ultimately unanswerable, especially given the considerable amount of time that has elapsed since Koch, Ademolli, and Scaramuzza designed their images. But the extraordinary overtness of some of the allusions suggests that, at least in those cases, Koch and his colleagues were indeed aware of their classical and medieval sources. And some of the intersections of medievalism and neo-classicism among those blatant allusions imply that, at least in those cases, the two approaches were, in fact, seen as compatible. Moreover, the wide variety of relationships encompassed by those intersections suggests that Koch and his colleagues did indeed view medievalism as extraordinarily flexible, as an approach that could coexist, incorporate, and even build on references to a style that has often been deemed its polar opposite. Thus, Koch and his colleagues present important evidence, not only for the nineteenth-century reception of the *Commedia* and for contemporaneous perceptions of the relationship between text and image, but also for the state of medievalism during the nineteenth century, and for the study of medievalism today.

Perhaps the clearest challenges to traditional distinctions between medievalism and neo-classicism are to be found in the engravings of Koch's *Commedia* drawings from approximately 1803 to 1825, for beneath the blatant classical and neo-classical references of these images, they are strikingly medieval.[5] Indeed, few early modern illustrations of Dante's text refer more thoroughly or more directly to medieval art than do those by Koch. For example, although the anonymous designer of a Venetian woodcut series from 1544 portrays Dante twice within his image of *Inferno* I, and thereby invokes the pre-modern device of continuous narrative, Koch depicts Dante three times in his illustration of this canto and thereby comes closer than the Venetian artist to, say, Cristoforo Cortese's five figures of Dante in a historiated initial of *Inferno* I from Nationale MS Fonds italien 78, which was executed during the first half of the fifteenth century, or to the six figures of Dante in the mid-fifteenth-century Sienese miniature of *Inferno* I from British Library MS Yates Thompson 36.[6] Moreover, even the Renaissance and Baroque artists who do depict Dante repeatedly in a single illustration do not show him curled up in sleep, as he is at the far left in Koch's image and in many of the medieval miniatures, such as a historiated initial in Musée Condé MS 597, which was probably illuminated by Buonamico Buffalmacco in 1327-28, and the opening image for the *Inferno* in Biblioteca Laurenziana MS Plutei 40.3, which was illustrated by an anonymous Sienese artist in approximately 1345.[7] Nor do any of the Renaissance and Baroque artists portray the Pilgrim shading his eyes when looking up at the hill whose shoulders were "clad in the rays of the planet that leads men aright by every path" (*Inf.* 1.17-18), as does the figure of Dante just to the right of Koch's sleeping figure and as does the Pilgrim in some of the *Commedia* miniatures, such as that executed in approximately 1440 by the *Vitae Imperatorum* Master for Bibliothèque Nationale MS Fonds italien 2017.[8] And, other than the master of the Venetian woodcuts, none of the Renaissance or Baroque illustrators shows Dante retreating to the left from a stack of the three beasts on a hillside at right, as he does in Koch's illustration and in most medieval miniatures of this canto.[9] Instead, most of the Renaissance and Baroque artists show Dante either retreating to the right, as in a 1506 woodcut from Florence, or somewhat surrounded by the three beasts, as in a drawing from 1587 by Jan van der Straet (also known as "Stradanus").[10] Thus, Koch seems to have derived his basic composition for this image from medieval rather than Renaissance or Baroque models.

The same could be said for much of Koch's iconography. For example, in portraying "the planet that leads men aright by every path," he departs from the

Renaissance tendencies either to ignore the planet, as in the 1506 woodcut of this canto, to depict it as a sunset with rays emanating from a hidden source, as in the 1544 woodcut of this scene, or, through oblique shadows, to merely hint at it being a sunset, as in the 1587 drawing by Stradanus. Instead, Koch joins Cortese and many other miniaturists in depicting the planet as an array of lines extending from an arc on the horizon.[11] Moreover, he comes close to the even more common medieval depiction of the planet as an array of lines emanating from a circle, as in both of the *Vitae Imperatorum* Master's images of this canto and in the frontispiece to a Florentine manuscript dating from 1419 and now preserved in the Vatican library as Vaticani Barberini latini 4112.[12]

Of course, not all of the subjects in Koch's illustration can be traced directly to *Commedia* miniatures, but even some of those subjects that do depart from them seem to descend from medieval iconography in general. For example, none of the plants in Koch's image have precise parallels in the medieval illustrations of Dante's text, but in their overt profusion, variety, and clarity, they do hint at having symbolic identities, at playing the same sort of iconographic role as do the flora in many pre-modern images, such as Martin Schongauer's engraving from circa 1475 of the Rest on the Flight into Egypt.[13] And though the lone sheep walking down a bright strip at the upper right of Koch's illustration is prefigured among *Commedia* images only by a rarely displayed, early fifteenth-century miniature on the opening page of the *Inferno* in Biblioteca Civica Gambalunga MS 4.I.II.25 at Rimini, that sheep is widely foreshadowed by medieval illustrations of Capricorn, such as that for the image of January in the famous *Très Riches Heures du Duc de Berry*.[14] Thus, like Koch's allusions to *Commedia* miniatures, his flora and fauna ground his illustration in the Middle Ages.

Those iconographic associations are polyvalently reinforced, moreover, by Koch's style. As noted above, some of the sixteenth-century illustrations of canto one, such as the Venetian woodcut from 1544, show more than one scene within a single image. But these illustrations are not typical of Renaissance or Baroque art and do not, in any case, have the unfolding, medieval appearance of Koch's engraving. His three figures of Dante have an almost cinematic quality as they narratively progress from the shadowy figure curled up in sleep at the far left, to the dazed figure shading his eyes at the near left, to the recoiling figure in the center of the image. Indeed, they recall the even greater movement of the five Dantes zigzagging up Cortese's illustration for this canto and of the six Dantes rising and falling in the Yates Thompson image of *Inferno* I. That is to say, they join some of the medieval miniatures in an overt primitivism that seems to assume a lack of sophistication on the part of the viewer.

The same could be said for Koch's characterization of animals. For example, the extremely pointed snout, flat skull, elongated neck, protruding ribs, and muscular haunches of the wolf, not to mention its rather serpentine tale, are closer to the features of the wolf on the opening page of the Gambalunga *Inferno* than to those of the wolf in any Renaissance or Baroque images of the Commedia, much less to the features of flesh-and-blood wolves. And the extraordinarily long neck of the oddly striped leopard, as well as its cylindrical body, are closer to those of the leopard in Madrid Biblioteca Nacional MS Vitrina 23-1, which was illuminated by an anonymous Florentine in the early fifteenth century, than to those of the leopard in, say, Stradanus's drawing of canto one, much less to those of actual leopards.[15] Moreover, the exceptionally profuse mane, curled lips, bear-like paws, and camel-like nose of Koch's lion resemble more those of its toy-like counterpart in Cortese's illustration of canto one than those of its counterpart in Renaissance or Baroque images of canto one, much less those of actual lions.

Yet, particularly in terms of linear articulation and spatial arrangement, Koch's three beasts are perhaps less medieval in their abstraction than are his plants. As mentioned earlier, his flora appear in such profusion and diversity that they would seem to have symbolic connotations, to be more than mere representations of the plants that Dante may have encountered in an Italian forest of 1300. Indeed, Koch's flora have such an unnatural crowding, particularly in the background on the left, and they feature so many striking juxtapositions, as in the pairing of a tall leafy plant and a low cluster of grass in the center foreground, that they directly recall the dense thickets of diverse flora in some fifteenth-century images, such as Schongauer's *Rest on the Flight into Egypt*. Moreover, despite the crowding among Koch's plants, they are often distinguished from each other in a manner that is common to Schongauer's engraving and to other pre-modern prints. For example, though Koch's flora are rarely so detailed as to differentiate each leaf or twig from its neighbor, almost every single one of them is, as a whole, crisply outlined, and some of them, such as the nearest tree at left, even participate in shadows that reinforce those borders and/or distinguish one group of flora from the next. Thus, the transitions among his plants are rarely as smooth as those in many Renaissance and Baroque images, such as Stradanus's drawing of canto one.

In part, those disruptures derive from Koch's invocation of medieval concessions to the nature of engraving, to the challenges in blending adjacent strokes in that medium. Technical advances during the seventeenth and eighteenth centuries, particularly in printing presses and in the durability of materials, had diminished the amount of surface area needed to maintain the integrity of a printing plate over the course of the publishing process. Yet many portions of Koch's illustration, such as the shading on the ground at the bottom of the image, return to the great gaps necessary between strokes in fifteenth-century engravings, such as Schongauer's *Rest on the Flight into Egypt*. Thus, Koch's illustration joins those of Schongauer and of other pre-modern artists in underscoring the linear nature of engraving. Indeed, in foregoing the nineteenth-century ability to locate those strokes closer together, Koch may foreground the linear nature of engraving to an even greater degree than do his late medieval predecessors, for they obviously had no such alternative.

Of course, in following pre-modern standards for the spacing of lines, Koch's illustration also eliminates many shades of gray, which in turn leads to anachronistically sharp distinctions in tone. Though rare passages of cross-hatching, as on the knoll between Virgil and the retreating Dante, suggest Koch anticipated at least some of his engraver's means for softening tonal transitions, he often avoids the need for such means and establishes sharp juxtapositions of black and white, as in the protagonists' drapery, or invites only crude transitions from one tonal extreme to another, as in the parallel lines forming shadows among the boughs at upper left, or skips shading altogether and defines his subjects through mere outline, as in some of the near flora and much of the background landscape. In other words, he deploys line and shade in such a manner as to establish dramatic shifts in tone, disjunctures that recall the lighting and technique of many works by Schongauer and other early engravers.

These disjunctures, like Koch's breaks between lines and between passages of flora, represent a revival rather than a continuation of pre-modern practices, for such dramatic shifts are almost entirely absent from most Renaissance and Baroque images of the *Commedia*. Stradanus, for example, has fairly smooth transitions from one line to the next and from one passage of strokes to the next or from one subject to the next. In fact, even where conventions of subject matter call for a break in Stradanus's composition, that break is usually accomplished by spatially and narratively plausible means, as in the lighting shift from the shadowy forest in the foreground of his illustration for *Inferno* I to the sunny hill in the middle ground of that image. Koch, on the other hand, distinguishes his two figures of Dante in the woods from his figure of Dante on the hill through a large and illogical diminution of size. He ignores the rules of perspectival consistency to create a spatial disjuncture that joins his sharp contrasts in tone, his breaks between lines, and his divisions among the flora in departing from not only his Renaissance and Baroque predecessors but also nineteenth-century conventions for verisimilitude.

Those disruptures, in turn, contribute to a general agitation that circulates throughout Koch's image and suffuses it with an expressiveness more typical of pre-modern than early modern images of the *Commedia*. Indeed, Koch so often echoes or even surpasses the expressionism of his pre-modern predecessors that he seems to have aspired to their extraordinary engagement with the *Commedia*. Perhaps more than any other nineteenth-century illustrator, except Blake or Doré, he seems to have noticed and adopted the passion with which many of the miniaturists portray Dante's text. Of course, that is not to say he agreed with common fourteenth-century claims that the *Commedia* is a true and accurate account of the afterlife.[16] But it is to suggest that, in accord with Romantic stereotypes of medieval art, he perceived the miniatures as reflections of an era when the faithful were extremely zealous in their religion and transparent in their expression of it. It is to suggest that he looked to the miniatures for not only the iconography and style of his *Commedia* cycle but also the overall tone of his illustrations, that he immersed his images in a spirit that he and many of his contemporaries believed to be medieval.

Yet, even as Koch anchored his illustrations in medievalism, he also invested them with obvious classical and neo-classical references. For example, the cut and design of Virgil's robe in the image of *Inferno* I are so close to ancient prototypes that they recall the extraordinary concern with sartorial accuracy in Jacques-Louis David's *Oath of the Horatii*, which famously derives its clothing directly from ancient models.[17] Moreover, like Dante's cloak, Virgil's robe seems so thick and weighty as to invoke not so much the light, dry appearance of clothing in many medieval images as the heavy, wet appearance of clothing in many ancient images. And Virgil's highly rhetorical, overtly contrappostal pose clearly descends from that of many figures in classical and neo-classical works, such as the nearest apostle on the left in Poussin's *Ordination* of 1647.[18] Thus, like some of the other passages in Koch's illustrations, Virgil blatantly invokes the style, models, and principles of classical and neo-classical art.

Indeed, to some degree, classical and neo-classical art are invoked by the overall composition for Koch's illustration of *Inferno* I. Like many protagonists in ancient art and its direct descendants, Koch's figure of the retreating Pilgrim is in the center of the image and forms a closely integrated unit with another figure, for other than the Pilgrim's left arm, his outline merges with that of Virgil to form a gentle trapezoid. Moreover, through the apparent exchange of gazes between Virgil and the Pilgrim and through the complements in their curves, that is, through the arc of Virgil's head and right arm as they accommodate the protrusion of Dante's right elbow and through the backwards sweep of Virgil's robe as it offsets Dante's right foot, the two figures establish a pictorial and psychological intersection, a harmony that embodies their narrative rapport and sets them off from the rest of the image. Of course, that is not to say they are completely isolated from the rest of the composition, for in accord with classical and neo-classical principles of art, the figure of Virgil is pictorially and thematically balanced by the stacking of the lion, leopard, and wolf at right. These three beasts lend the composition a lateral symmetry that is echoed by, among other elements, the full tree at the upper left and the bank of cliffs at the upper right. Moreover, they extend the trapezoid constituted by Dante and Virgil into a roughly equilateral pyramid, particularly via the head and neck of the leopard and of the lion. That is to say, they join Virgil and Dante in establishing a highly stable, geometric anchor at the center of the composition, in emulating the main subjects of many classical and neo-classical works.

Nor are they the only fundamental aspects of the image to play on the expectations of viewers who have had significant exposure to classical and/or neo-classical art, for despite the overt naiveté of many principles and passages in the image, it is steeped in some common early nineteenth-century tenets for verisimilitude. For example, the central figures have the proportions relative to each other that the viewer might expect from the figures' flesh-and-blood counterparts. Moreover, the landscape generally adheres to the principles of one-point perspective. Additionally, although shading is not uniform throughout the image and may not be particularly convincing in many passages, the depiction of volume and relief often provides at least some consistency of depth and spatial relativity. Indeed, the preponderance of shadows on the right side of the figures and of the setting in the foreground strongly suggests that there is a single, bright light beyond the frame at left, one that overwhelms both the diffused rays emanating from the setting planet and the local illumination from the moon, the stars, and the stripe down which the sheep descends. Thus, the image as a whole is fairly unified and somewhat in tune with neo-classical standards for realistic representation of the world outside of its borders.

In fact, even when Koch's illustrations overtly depart from neo-classical principles for verisimilitude, they sometimes do so through emulation of classical works or of the spiritual heirs to those works. For instance, in depicting the Heavenly Ladies giving encouragement to Virgil in canto two of the *Inferno*, Koch invokes Raphael's *Disputa*, which was executed from approximately 1509 to 1510.[19] Both artists depict a semi-circle of symmetrically disposed figures floating on clouds beneath an arched frame and above a balanced arrangement of terrestrial figures. Indeed, Virgil's pose closely parallels that of the bearded figure just to the right of the altar in the *Disputa*, while Dante's pose, particularly his right arm, approaches that of the young man leaning forward in the middle of the group to the left of the altar. Thus, Koch punctuates his predominantly medieval approach with classical and neo-classical allusions that operate on many different levels of style, composition, and iconography.

Like punctuation, Koch's classical and Renaissance references sometimes play integral roles in the meaning and tone of his work, for, in addition to endowing his illustrations with a distinguished lineage, they often invest critical details and subthemes with characteristics that had long been specifically associated with classical and/or Renaissance culture. For example, insofar as ancient art is associated with extraordinarily profound and cool rationalism, particularly in confronting the vicissitudes of life, the classical aspects of Virgil's figure underscore one of the main virtues that he supposedly manifests as Dante's guide through Hell, particularly when, as in this illustration, the Pilgrim turns to him for refuge from the three beasts in *Inferno* I. And to the degree that Raphael's art revolves around the *grazia* with which Vasari and subsequent critics often associate it, Koch's allusions to *The Disputa* suggest that the Heavenly Ladies in canto two of the *Inferno* do indeed embody the grace and elegance with which Dante associates them.[20] Thus, by means of classical and Renaissance references, Koch overtly drives home points vital to a pictorial narrative that is otherwise fundamentally medieval in origin and spirit. In other words, he pursues a medievalism that dominates his *Commedia* illustrations yet easily accommodates neoclassical themes and references, indeed, that builds juxtapositions with those themes and references to reinforce his medieval expressiveness elsewhere in the images.

In contrast, Ademolli's *Commedia* illustrations, which were apparently designed shortly before they were engraved by Lasinio Figlio in 1817, adhere so closely to the principles and examples of ancient art that even the most medieval episodes in those images are ultimately cast in thoroughly neo-classical terms.[21] For instance, the engraving of Ademolli's drawing for *Inferno* XXV tackles a bolgia whose contents as a whole epitomize early nineteenth-century stereotypes of the Middle Ages, for Dante claims that, as Virgil and the Pilgrim pass by the eighth pocket of the seventh circle, they observe a nest of serpents attacking thieves in several horrific and highly imaginative ways.[22] Indeed, few other scenes in Dante's underworld are as fantastic or dramatic as are those of the first and last thieves encountered by the Pilgrim. In brief but graphic terms, Dante describes the first robber, Vanni Fucci, being seized by a lizard, set afire, reduced to ash, and restored to human form for yet another such attack (*Inf.* 24.97-120). In much greater and even more graphic detail, Dante describes two of the last three robbers being slowly and painfully transmogrified into serpents (*Inf.* 25.49-135). Yet, unlike Koch and the miniaturists, whose images of *Inferno* XXIV-XXV revolve around the transformation of those two thieves, Ademolli focuses on a cameo appearance in canto twenty-five by the centaur Cacus, a relatively brief and banal subject described by Dante in far more laconic terms than those employed for the immolation of Fucci or the transmogrification of the thieves (*Inf.* 25.17-34). In other words, Ademolli foregoes two highly imaginative and dynamic scenes of Dante's contemporaries to concentrate on a tableau of Cacus being encircled by a dragon, on a comparatively static and conventional subject from classical mythology.

Moreover, Ademolli portrays one of the more sedate moments from the Cacus episode, for although Dante mentions that the centaur ran away shortly after Virgil and the Pilgrim first spotted him, and although Dante notes that the dragon "sets on fire whomever it encounters," Ademolli depicts Cacus neither fleeing nor being set ablaze by his attacker.[23] Instead, he shows little more than the dragon beginning to wrap itself around Cacus. Indeed, though the twist of the centaur's neck, like his raised hooves, may join the electrified hair and gaping mouths of his companions in suggesting their distress, these implications are mild in comparison to the horror of the events about to unfold. That is to say, Ademolli concentrates on a scene that is essentially one of foreboding, on a moment in which the dragon is merely getting a firmer grip and a better angle for an assault that has not yet happened. Thus, despite the fact that the snakes burgeoning from Cacus's back may be so graphic as to invoke medievalist values, the most classical subject of the Pilgrim's encounter with the thieves is largely portrayed in harmony with the neo-classical preference for understated implication over graphic detail, for the mere suggestion of violence over explicit description of it.

Nor is that the end of classical influence on this work, for Ademolli overtly bases his composition on the ancient statue of Laocoön by Athanadoros, Hagesandros, and Polydoros of Rhodes.[24] Ademolli has cast Cacus as Laocoön, converted the snakes assaulting Laocoön to a winged dragon, added serpents emerging from the protagonist's back, portrayed the figure at right as a snake from the waist down, and added two victims at the far left. But the basic configuration of his engraving is virtually identical to that of the *Laocoön*, for both works depict a mature male flanked by youths sharing the protagonist's struggle with a nest of giant serpents. Moreover, like the sculptors of the *Laocoön*, Ademolli also portrays the two young men who are nearest the protagonist turning towards the latter, while the protagonist himself gazes out toward the viewer. And, again like the *Laocoön* sculptors, Ademolli depicts the main figure in a sharply twisting pose with one arm reaching back and up while the other arm reaches down and forward. Indeed, Ademolli approximates the *Laocoön* so closely that his engraving seems more concerned with stating his own artistic sources and values than with conveying the spirit of Dante's text.

In fact, Ademolli otherwise adheres so closely to the artistic language of classicism and neo-classicism, if not a specific model from those approaches, that he does indeed seem to displace the drama and immediacy of the *Commedia* with historical allusion for its own sake. While Koch positions the first transmogrifying thief—his main figure for this bolgia—on the left side of his pen drawing for canto twenty-five, Ademolli joins many ancient artists and their spiritual heirs in locating his main figures at the very center of his image, for the neck of the dragon is almost as far from the top of the frame as the hooves of Cacus are from the bottom of the frame, and the tail of the centaur is almost as far from the left side of the image as his left hoof is from the right side of the image.[25] Thus, Cacus and his attacker constitute a core around which the rest of the composition revolves.

Moreover, like the protagonists in many classical and neo-classical images, as well as in Koch's illustration of *Inferno* I, Cacus and the dragon participate in a roughly equilateral triangle, for, in conjunction with the first curve in the tail of the youth at right, Cacus's left hoof complements the curve in his own tail and joins it in leading up to a third, nearly equidistant curve in the neck of the dragon. Admittedly, the diagonal formed by the dragon's mid-section and left wing, as well as by the right arm and lower half of Cacus, is interrupted by the dragon's right wing, which continues the diagonal thrust of the youth at right and of Cacus's torso. However, as that right wing extends beyond the dragon's body and into the upper left corner of the image, it is to some degree offset not only by the left hand of the youth at right, as that hand protrudes towards the upper right corner of the image, and by the head of the dragon, as that head extends well over the youth at right, but also by the symmetry of all four youths flanking Cacus, for, although there are three young men to the left of Cacus and only one to his right, the fuller exposure of the figure at right somewhat compensates for that numerical discrepancy and reinforces the lateral balance of the composition.

That configuration of the composition is part of an overt, overall rhetoricization of the image, a pictorial manipulation that, in both principle and character, is closely in tune with classical beliefs and is, as in many ancient works, perhaps most manifest in the idealization of the figures. Though the lumpy triceps of Cacus's left arm reveal that Ademolli did not always have a firm grasp on anatomy, he seems to have at least attempted to invoke classical standards of corporeal beauty and elegance. Whereas the flesh on Koch's thief is mangled and distorted by the claws of his attacker, Ademolli's Cacus is apparently unscathed by the dragon's talons, and he has not yet been seized by its tail. And while Koch's thief bends over backwards and twists almost ninety degrees in a desperate, ungainly attempt to escape his attacker, Cacus and the other thieves in Ademolli's illustration contort just enough to flex their muscles without distorting them or their bodies as a whole. Thus, they strike dynamic poses that convey poise and elegance while underscoring the Herculean dimensions of Cacus's upper body and the leaner, but no less ideal, proportions of the centaur's fellow victims.

Not surprisingly, the idealization of Ademolli's figures, and, in fact, of his illustration as a whole, is to a great degree built on contemporaneous standards of verisimilitude, particularly Neo-classical principles of mimesis. Indeed, in echoing the world beyond the frame of Ademolli's illustration, Cacus and his fellow thieves often go far beyond the minimum criteria of those principles. For example, the bestial nature of Cacus is underscored by the prominence of his chest hair, by the porcine dimensions of his nose, and by the heaviness of his brow, while the taxonomy, beauty, and perhaps danger of the semi-serpent at right are embodied by the comparatively detailed and otherwise superfluous delineation of the muscles in his torso and of the scales on his tail. That is to say, Ademolli has labored over minutiae that convey the values associated with the extra-narrative counterparts of his subjects, and, at least in these details, he approaches the nearly infinite data that constitute the whole of those counterparts.

Ademolli also makes an effort to endow his subjects with the substance that might be expected of their extra-narrative counterparts. Although the youths at left, as well as Virgil and Dante, are defined primarily by line, all of the figures in the image eclipse each other in an order and to a degree that is apparently consistent with their relative depth in the image. Moreover, Cacus, the youth at right, and the serpents seem to have volume, for they cast shadows on the ground and the right side of their contours is consistently darker and thicker than the left side of their contours. In other words, they seem to be opaque and take up space, to join the other figures and the setting in fulfilling at least some early nineteenth-century criteria for verisimilitude.

Of course, in so doing, they and the other figures may underscore the artifice of the image and concomitantly accentuate the participation of the artist in its production, for the construction of any attempt at mimesis may be highlighted if that effort is seen as falling short of fully realizing its goal.[26] Yet it is perhaps through Ademolli's departures from, rather than his adherence to, early nineteenth-century standards of verisimilitude that he most directly and most obviously accentuates his participation in the illustrations. Indeed, in accord with Renaissance and Mannerist strategies for underscoring the artist's contributions to a work, for conveying classical and Renaissance esteem for individuality and self-expression, Ademolli sometimes literally and figuratively foregrounds his line.[27] For example, he delineates much of the main serpent, particularly the top of its upper torso, with conspicuously long and unbroken contours, with lines recalling the virtuoso "O" that Vasari claims Giotto drew for a patron demanding proof of his talent, or the extraordinarily long and sinuous contours of Botticelli's figures.[28] And, especially in the direction and width of his strokes, he sometimes departs from the prevailing practices elsewhere in the illustration. For instance, he occasionally has lines representing shading or internal definition transcend otherwise sacrosanct borders, as in the torso of the main serpent, or he has lines grow thicker or thinner to a degree that is irrational in relationship to the width of neighboring contours, as is true for the strokes constituting the slight hill just beneath Cacus's right rear hoof.

Thus, while Koch departs from Neo-classical standards of verisimilitude more often than he adheres to them, and while he does so in a wide array of systematic ways that either participate directly in a medievalist approach or invoke Antique values that reinforce his medieval narrative, Ademolli departs from Neo-classical standards of verisimilitude just often enough for those departures to stand out as exceptions to the rule. Moreover, he does so almost exclusively through such large and detailed references to earlier works that those allusions are not easily overlooked or through exceptionally direct evidence of his physical participation in the production of the work. Indeed, Ademolli departs from Neo-classical standards of verisimilitude in such personal and blatant ways that, even as he betrays those standards, he invokes classical and Renaissance esteem for individuality and self-expression. Moreover, the disrupture of those departures, which in their abruptness invite association with the explicit disjunctures of medieval art and of early nineteenth-century medievalism, are to some degree veiled, or at least counterbalanced, by the overt classicism of such famously ancient sources as the *Laocoön* and by the Renaissance and Mannerist roots of Ademolli's graphic indications of his contribution to the image. Consequently, in adapting classical sources and their heirs for bravura departures from neo-classical standards of verisimilitude, Ademolli does not undermine the overall Neo-classical tenor of his illustration and may even reinforce its tendency towards being more of a calculated study in illusion and allusion than a close representation of a highly emotional and imaginative text.

Scaramuzza, on the other hand, is expressive on a scale and in a manner that closely accord with nineteenth-century medievalist values, yet do not depart from, and in some ways even build on, many of the same neo-classical principles found in Ademolli's images.[29] In the hundreds of *Commedia* drawings that Scaramuzza executed in the three decades prior to their publication in 1865, he does not copy the compositions and iconography of classical and Renaissance art nearly as fully, frequently, or literally as does Ademolli. But in many ways he does invoke the tone of many ancient and Renaissance works. For example, the standard-bearer at left in his drawing of the cowards echoes the light-footed grace of the angel in the center of Raphael's *Expulsion of Heliodorus*, as both figures dash on tip-toe across the scene.[30] And Scaramuzza's crowd of cowards as a whole recalls the extraordinarily complex interplay of figures in many classical and Renaissance paintings, such as Titian's *Bacchus and Ariadne*.[31] Indeed, Scaramuzza constructs a perpendicular tableau of nudes who so thoroughly overlap and are, at times, so closely intertwined that they constitute as much an organic whole as a parade of individuals. Moreover, the triangle formed by those figures is hardly less regular in its geometry than is, say, the triangle of maenads and satyrs in *Bacchus and Ariadne*, for the top of Scaramuzza's crowd is nearly equal in length and in the angle of its departure from the hypotenuse of the cowards, as is the bottom of that crowd. Thus, Scaramuzza's overall composition has the blatant unity and overt control that were highly prized by classical and neo-classical critics.

Those properties of the cowards as a whole, moreover, revolve around a diamond established in the middle of the image by a falling youth and a balding man with a long beard. Just below a dramatic column of shade on a back wall of the cavernous setting, the arms of the young man merge with the head and beard of the older man to form the upper left side of the diamond. They are paralleled by a diagonal formed to their lower right from the right leg of the youth and the left leg of the older man. And both of those lines are intersected at nearly right angles by the lower edge of the young man's torso and by the upper edge of the older man's torso. Consequently, Scaramuzza's illustration accords with classical and neo-classical encouragement to anchor compositions around centrally located, geometrically regular forms.

Indeed, Scaramuzza's diamond serves as a fulcrum for a plethora of symmetries that represent another value often promoted by neo-classical critics and frequently found in ancient and Renaissance art—balance. In terms of lighting and distribution of participants, the crowd of cowards is weighted towards the right, towards the darkest and densest mass of figures, but in terms of lateral length, the triangle of sinners is almost evenly divided by the falling youth and the bearded older man, for the cowards race from the right edge of the image to a bright space just beyond the foreground wall at far left. Thus, the diamond serves as a midpoint for the flow of visible figures as a whole. Moreover, although that flow is privileged by the right-to-left tapering of the triangle and by the sprinting figure of the standard bearer at far left, the diagonal formed by the lower edge of the triangle, particularly by the body and pole of the standard bearer, is to some degree offset by the diagonal formed by the sinners in the right foreground as they twist and reach back to the upper right. And, though the dark silhouettes of Virgil and Dante weigh down the lower left corner of the image, they are somewhat balanced by the dark mass of cowards at the upper right. Thus, in accord with perhaps the most widespread stereotypes of classical and neo-classical art, Scaramuzza's illustration is not only centered but also polyvalently and emphatically balanced.

Of course, as may be obvious from even a quick glance at the image, it is to a great degree also constructed from highly idealized bodies that closely adhere to ancient and Renaissance principles of anatomical perfection. Indeed, though the cowards' faces are often so idiosyncratic as to seem like portraits, many of their bodies are rather generic in their approximation of classical standards for perfect muscle development, definition, and proportion. For example, the two highly contorted figures in the right foreground are nearly identical in the length of their limbs, the hypertrophy of their physique, and the leanness that facilitates the visibility of their muscle development. Moreover, in defiance of ageist stereotypes, the balding man who clutches one of his own legs in mid-stride not only exhibits outstanding agility but also joins the two foreground figures in the proportions, muscularity, and clarity of his anatomy. Of course, that is not to say that all of the males in the image share the same Herculean build as those three figures, for some of the young men, such as the falling figure in the center of the image and the standard-bearer at left, are substantially thinner in build and smoother in surface than the balding man and the two contortionists in the foreground. Yet even the less muscular males in the image often embody classical ideals, for, given the evident youth of these beardless figures, their comparatively lean physiques accord with the ancient esteem for "decorum," for appropriate accommodation of different circumstances.[32]

In fact, from a classical perspective, the standard-bearer's comparatively svelte build is appropriate twice over, as he appears to be not only youthful but, like Raphael's central angel from the *Expulsion of Heliodorus*, also an embodiment of superhuman grace, a divine agent whose mission calls for a light step and exquisite balance. Thus, Scaramuzza joins Raphael and other neo-classical artists in not only idealizing his subjects but also doing so according to many of the same values promoted by those artists, in pursuing the same paradigms of physical perfection.

If the rhetorical spirit of that aestheticization or of Scaramuzza's compositional manipulation is noticed, it also invokes classicism by literally and figuratively foregrounding the artist's contributions to the image. But it does not reflect the artist's hand as directly as do Ademolli's exceptionally long and transgressive lines. Nor does it reflect the artist's sources as specifically as does Ademolli's allusion to the *Laocoön* or as polyvalently as do Koch's many iconographic, technical, and stylistic references to classical, neo-classical, and medieval art. In fact, Scaramuzza's rhetoricization of the image is hardly more direct in foregrounding him than is his adherence to nineteenth-century principles of verisimilitude, for he invokes those principles so fully that he underscores his artistry to an extraordinary degree.

At the most fundamental level, Scaramuzza plays to nineteenth-century standards of verisimilitude by avoiding many of the artificial terms in which this episode could be portrayed. Although he idealizes his image in some ways, he does not do so in all ways, and even when he does do so, he rarely departs from the realm of possibility. For example, though the muscularity and grace of his figures may be scarce outside of this illustration, they are not impossible among flesh-and-blood human beings. Indeed, given that many of Scaramuzza's figures differ from each other in the virtues that they seem to embody, they may not collectively depart from at least a portion of an equally active and comparably youthful crowd outside of this illustration. Nor, given the premise that the cowards are desperately pursuing a banner they will never catch and perhaps even more desperately striving to escape a swarm of stinging insects, do those sinners greatly depart from the collective form many other people might take in similar circumstances. In fact, it seems quite likely that any group of individuals who do not share exactly the same size, stamina, and speed would form a collective triangle as they race after a common goal and/or from a common threat. Moreover, those figures are set in a spacious cavern that is not unlike many that may be found in the Apennines and other terrestrial mountain ranges. Finally, both the setting and the figures are consistently lit from the left in accord with the openings to the cavern; indeed, the play of light is partly articulated through an exceptionally meticulous matching of depicted surfaces to the texture of their counterparts outside the illustration. For example, the ground is largely defined through short strokes that suggest a scaly bed of sedimentary rock, whereas the comparatively smooth skin of the sinners is conveyed through soft stippling and a slight smudging of ink. Thus, by mid-nineteenth-century standards, Scaramuzza's illustration is highly mimetic and constitutes an overt declaration of his participation in its construction.

Yet, although Scaramuzza's extraordinary adherence to nineteenth-century principles of verisimilitude may foreground him to a great degree, it also facilitates many of the more medievalist aspects of his image, for they often profit from the illusion of a pictorial realm that seems discrete from, yet compatible with, the world outside of the frame. In fact, the image invites the viewer to slip into the fiction without disrupting the integrity of the narrative, to fully immerse him- or herself as a participant in the depicted events, for, instead of explicitly treating the viewer as a transgressive figure, instead of, say, confronting him or her with a trace of the artist's hand or with a direct gaze from one of the figures, Scaramuzza hides his artistry and has his figures seem to ignore the viewer. He creates a world that is so much like the one outside of its borders as to foster a sense of continuity between those realms, yet he ignores that continuity so thoroughly that he not only avoids reinforcing the role of the viewer as an extra-narrative observer, but also allows the latter to project him- or herself into the scene and even to identify with one or more of the figures.[33] Thus, rather than observe a suffering sinner from the pictorial equivalent of a distant, second-person role, as may result from the ocular dialogue ostensibly proffered by the direct gaze from Ademolli's Cacus, the viewer is invited to collapse his or her third-person identity as an observer with a first-person empathy for the characters, for figures who resemble humans outside of this image and inhabit a realm not unlike some terrestrial settings.[34]

Moreover, in accord with nineteenth-century medievalist tendencies, the danger and suffering to which the viewer would be exposed in identifying with the cowards is underscored by the exceptional expressiveness with which those sinners futilely pursue the banner at left and flee their biting and stinging pursuers. For example, though none of Scaramuzza's figures exceed the general limits of human flexibility, many of the cowards, particularly those in the right foreground, at least test those limits, for they bend over backwards and/or twist sideways to extraordinary degrees as they try to brush away the insects behind them. Moreover, their desperation is further, and perhaps more finely, articulated by their faces, for though their furrowed brows, bulging eyes, and gaping mouths may not betray the precise emotion of each figure, they leave little doubt that the cowards are in great distress and thoroughly caught up in the passion of the moment. Indeed, the cowards are shown in perhaps the most passionate scene of the episode. Unlike Ademolli, who shows Cacus at one of the tamer moments during his brief appearance in Dante's narrative, Scaramuzza shows the cowards in the full misery of their ongoing suffering and at the moment when that torment is, perhaps, first made evident to the

Pilgrim, when the latter gets his first close view of the procession. In other words, rather than merely hinting at the suffering of the cowards, Scaramuzza adheres to nineteenth-century principles of medievalism by graphically depicting the climax of the action in the scene and of the protagonist's full realization of its horror.

As part of that tendency, Scaramuzza shows the cowards from a distance that is close enough to allow clear perception of the nearest sinners' particular torments and individual responses, yet far enough to register the tremendous number of cowards and thereby articulate the enormity of collective suffering in this portion of the narrative. Moreover, he dramatizes the sinners' plight through exceptionally sharp juxtapositions of tone, as shafts of light seem to shoot across the top and bottom of the cowardly crowd while leaving the middle figures almost lost in shadow. Thus, the suffering of the nearest sinners is highlighted, and the great emotion represented by their poses and facial expressions is tonally projected onto the image as a whole. Of course, in thereby articulating medievalist values via a pictorial language that incorporates many principles of verisimilitude and other forms of neo-classical rhetoric, Scaramuzza suggests that he did not perceive those means and ends as strictly antithetical. Indeed, the subtlety and thoroughness with which he deploys neo-classicism in the promotion of medievalism implies that he may not even have seen those means as historical allusions, much less as descending from a different period than that which may have given rise to his ends. Instead, he may have seen his means as merely the most efficient way of communicating a *Commedia* interpretation that, as much as it may embody nineteenth-century medievalism, is ultimately unique.

In any case, Scaramuzza's historical references are certainly far less overt than those of Koch. The latter joins Scaramuzza in deploying neo-classical principles for images that promote medievalist ends, but Koch's ends do not build as directly or completely on neo-classicism as do those of Scaramuzza. Instead, they build to a great degree on medieval means that largely co-exist with a much smaller set of neo-classical allusions, with a group of compositional and iconographic references to ancient and Renaissance models that have rather blatant relevance to the narrative. In fact, the overall spirit of Koch's illustration builds so closely on medieval models and medieval principles—and so many of those references are no less overt than his neo-classical allusions—that an obvious juxtaposition is established between the two sets of references, a blatant contrast that almost paradoxically fosters two means by which the neo-classical references indirectly reinforce the medievalism of the illustration. First, in representing sharp historical and pictorial disjunctures, the blatant juxtaposition of allusions conforms to nineteenth-century perceptions of medieval art as having a naiveté that includes not only overt disruptures in, or a total lack of, standards of representation for an image, but also obvious departures in those standards and/or exceptions from consistent representation of the world outside their frame. Second, as Koch's classicism represents historical allusions that are overt but less pervasive than his medievalism, that classicism foregrounds the blatancy and pre-eminence of his medievalism in shaping the meaning and tone of the image as a whole. Thus, Koch plays these two sets of allusions off each other so expertly and so overtly that he leaves little doubt he was aware of not only their referentiality but also the common perception that those two types of allusion, as well as the two milieux to which they refer, are antithetical.

Ademolli, on the other hand, seems to ignore that polarity, as he repeatedly bypasses opportunities for medieval expression and dwells instead on overt neo-classical references. Although illustrating a text that was widely perceived during the nineteenth century as a paradigm of medieval literature, and although tackling episodes that are among the most conducive in the *Commedia* to the medievalist fascination with the sublime and grotesque, Ademolli favors the most classical and sedate subjects in those episodes. Moreover, he orients his illustrations so thoroughly around classical models—and those models have so little connection to Dante's narrative—that he seems more concerned with underscoring his artistic values and influences than with conveying the *Commedia*. Consequently, he departs from Scaramuzza in leaving little doubt that he was aware of his historical sources and of nineteenth-century claims that those sources are incompatible with medieval art, but, unlike Koch, he does not overtly exploit this perceived incompatibility to directly promote his interpretation of the *Commedia*. Instead, he presents a third approach to art-historical allusion and thereby demonstrates the great range with which this trope was viewed during the nineteenth century. That is to say, he joins Koch and Scaramuzza in undermining the stereotyping of nineteenth-century medievalism and in encouraging greater and more detailed study of its many manifestations.

TOWSON UNIVERSITY

NOTES

[1] An earlier version of this paper was delivered at the Nineteenth International Conference on Medievalism, October 2, 2004 at the University of New Brunswick in Fredericton, Canada.

[2] "*Commedia* Images in the Neo-Gothic Age(s)," *Studies in Medievalism* XV (forthcoming).

[3] For general introductions to nineteenth-century *Commedia* illustrations, see Alfred Bassermann, *Dantes Spuren in Italien* (Munich: Oldenbourg, 1898); Ludwig Volkmann, *Iconografia dantesca* (London: Grevel, 1899); Jean-Pierre Barricelli, *Dante's Vision and the*

Artist (New York: Peter Lang, 1992); Eugene Paul Nassar, *Illustrations to Dante's "Inferno"* (Rutherford, NJ: Fairleigh Dickinson UP, 1994); Ralph Pite, "Illustrating Dante," in *The Circle of Our Vision: Dante's Presence in English Romantic Poetry* (Oxford: Clarendon Press, 1994), 39-67; and Charles H. Taylor and Patricia Finley, *Images of the Journey in Dante's "Divine Comedy"* (New Haven and London: Yale UP, 1997). For more monographic yet general sources on Koch, Ademolli, and Scaramuzza, as well as for specific sources on their *Commedia* images, see the bibliographies in the notes below.

[4]Note that, other than when referring to the late eighteenth- and early nineteenth-century movement that sought to deliberately revive classical art, I do not capitalize the term "neo-classical" in this paper and shall presume it to encompass all classically inflected art dating after the fifth century C.E., including art of the Italian Renaissance and Baroque periods. The literature on the properties of neo-classical art is vast, surprisingly uniform for its size, and, within the field of art history, fairly well-known. For scholars from other fields who wish more information on those properties, particularly on those I mention below, an excellent starting point is still Hugh Honour's *Neo-classicism* (1968; rev. ed. New York: Penguin, 1977).

[5]For more on Koch and his *Commedia* illustrations, see Francis Xavier Kraus, *Dante* (Berlin: G. Grote'sche Verlagsbuchhandlung, 1897); Volkmann; Emilio Valle, ed. *Iconografia Dantesca del pittore Giuseppe Antonio Koch* (Valdagno: Giovanni Galla, 1904); Ernest Jaffé, *Joseph Anton Koch: Sein Leben und sein Schaffen* (Innsbruck: Wagner, 1905); Guglielmo Locella, *Dante's Francesca Da Rimini in der Literatur, Bildenden Kunst und Musik* (Eszlingen: Paul Neff Verlag, 1913); V. A. Dirksen, *Joseph Anton Koch* (Hamburg: Hamburger Kunsthalle, 1920); *Joseph Anton Koch (1768-1839): Gemälde und Zeichnungen*, exh. cat. Berlin, January-March 1939 (Berlin: National-Galerie, 1939); R. von Otto Lutterotti, *Joseph Anton Koch, 1768-1839, mit Werkverzeichnis und Briefen des Künstlers* (Berlin: Deutscher Verein für Kunstwissenschaft, 1940; repr. Vienna: Herold, 1985); the entry for Koch in the *Enciclopedia dantesca*, ed. Umberto Bosco, 6 vols. (Rome: Istituto della Enciclopedia Italiana, 1970-78); Bertel Thorvaldsen, *Dante, Vergil, Geryon: der 17. Höllengesang der Göttlichen Komödie in der bildenden Kunst* (Stuttgart: Stattsgalerie Stuttgart, 1980); Corrado Gizzi, *Koch e Dante* (Milan: Mazzotta, 1988); and Nassar.

[6]For the Venetian woodcut and Koch's illustration, see Nassar, pp. 37 and 59, respectively. For Cortese's illustration and the Bibliothèque Nationale miniature, see *Illuminated Manuscripts of the "Divine Comedy"*. ed. Peter Brieger, Millard Meiss, and Charles Singleton, 2 vols. (Princeton: Princeton UP, 1969), II, pls. 45a and 45b, respectively. Unless otherwise noted, I have derived my attributions of the miniatures from the catalogue by Brieger and Meiss in *Illuminated Manuscripts of the "Divine Comedy"*, I, 209-339. For a catalogue of almost all known *Commedia* manuscripts, see Marcella Roddewig, *Dante Alighieri, "Die göttliche Komödie": Vergleichende Bestandsaufnahme der "Commedia"-Handschriften* (Stuttgart: A. Hiersemann, 1984).

[7]For the Musée Condé and Plutei miniatures, see *Illuminated Manuscripts . . .* , II, pls. 6b and 7, respectively. Note that Meiss's case for attributing the Musée Condé miniatures to an artist in Francesco Traini's orbit has been eroded by Luciano Bellosi's documentary and stylistic evidence in *Buffalmacco e il "Trionfo della Morte"* (Turin: Simonelli, 1974), which convincingly argues that Buonamico Buffalmacco executed the closely related Camposanto frescoes in Pisa. For strong arguments against Meiss's dating of the

manuscript to approximately 1345, which he seems to have largely based on Francesco Mazzoni's "Guido da Pisa interprete di Dante e la sua fortuna presso il Boccaccio," *Studi Danteschi* XXXV (1958), 29-128, see Bruno Sandkühler's *Die frühen Dantekommentare und ihr Verhältnis zur mittelalterlichen Kommentartradition*, Münchner Romanistiche Arbeiten XIX (Munich: W. Fink, 1967), esp. 163, which argues that the text must have been written between 1325 and 1333, and probably between 1325 and 1328; L. Jenaro-MacLennan's "The Dating of Guido da Pisa's Commentary on the *Inferno*," *Italian Studies* XXIII (1968), 19-54, which argues for a dating of 1327-28; and Enzo Orvieto's "Guido da Pisa e il commento inedito all'*Inferno* dantesco: Le chiose al trentatresimo canto," *Italica* XLVI (1969), 17-32, which claims that the manuscript must have been finished by 1328. See also Mazzoni's unconvincing reply to Jenaro-MacLennan in Mazzoni's entry on Guido da Pisa for the *Enciclopedia dantesca*.

[8]For the *Vitae Imperatorum* Master's miniature, see *Illuminated Manuscripts . . .* , II, pl. 46a. All references to the *Commedia* are based on Giorgio Petrocchi's four-volume edition *La "Commedia" secondo l'antica vulgata* (Milan: Mondadori, 1966-68). All translations of the *Commedia* are from Charles Singleton's three-volume edition (Princeton: Princeton UP, 1970-75).

[9]See, for examples, the first image accompanying the body of Guido da Pisa's *Inferno* commentary in Musée Condé MS 597 (*Illuminated Manuscripts . . .* , II, pl. 39) and the opening page for the *Inferno* in Biblioteca Nacional MS Vitrina 23-2 at Madrid, a work that was illustrated by an anonymous Florentine in approximately 1415 (*Illuminated Manuscripts . . .* , II, pl. 15).

[10]For the 1506 woodcut and Stradanus's drawing, see Nassar, pp. 36 and 38, respectively.

[11]For the Cortese image, see *Illuminated Manuscripts . . .* , II, pl. 45a, as noted above.

[12]For the first of the two miniatures by the *Vitae Imperatorum* Master, see *Illuminated Manuscripts . . .* , II, pl. 46a, as noted above. For the second of the Master's miniatures and for the Vatican miniature, see *Illuminated Manuscripts . . .* , II, pls. 46b and 12b, respectively.

[13]For Schongauer's engraving, see James Snyder's *Northern Renaissance Art: Painting, Sculpture, the Graphic Arts from 1350 to 1575* (Englewood Cliffs, NJ and New York: Prentice-Hall, Inc. and Harry N. Abrams, Inc., 1985), fig. 287.

[14]For the Gambalunga miniature, see *Illuminated Manuscripts . . .* , II, pl. 8b. For the image of January in the *Très Riches Heures du Duc de Berry*, see Snyder, pl. 10.

[15]For the Madrid miniature, see *Illuminated Manuscripts . . .* , II, pl. 11.

[16]For cursory overviews of the manner in which fourteenth-century commentators treated Dante's claims to truth and authority, see Vittorio Rossi, *Scritti di critica letteraria* (Florence: G. C. Sansoni, 1930), esp. I, 293-332; Dino Mattalìa, "Dante Alighieri," in *I classici italiani nell storia della critica*, ed. Walter Binni, 3 vols. (Florence: L. S. Olschki, 1954) I, 3-93; and Siro A. Chimenz, *Dante*, Letteratura italiana, I Maggiori (Milan: Carlo Marzorati, 1956), 70-103. For a two-paragraph overview of the manner in which all fourteenth- and fifteenth-century commentators perceived Dante's claims to truth and authority, see Peter Brieger, "Pictorial Commentaries to the *Commedia*," in *Illuminated Manuscripts of the "Divine Comedy"*, 88-90. And for a more extended discussion of differences in those perceptions between the fourteenth and fifteenth centuries, as well

as for an analysis of the degree to which *Commedia* miniaturists echoed those shifts, see my articles "Historicizing the *Divine Comedy*: Renaissance Responses to a 'Medieval' Text," *Medievalism: The Year's Work* XV (2000), 83-106, esp. 94; and "Early Modern Responses to Dante's Authority: Iconoclasm in Illuminated Manuscripts of the *Divine Comedy*," *Manuscripta* XLV/XLVI (2001/2002), 25-48, esp. 37-48.

[17]For the *Oath of the Horatii*, see almost any survey of Western art, such as the twelfth edition of Fred S. Kleiner and Christin J. Mamiya's *Gardner's Art through the Ages* (Belmont, CA: Thompson/Wadsworth, 2005), fig. 28-21.

[18]For Poussin's painting, see the fourth edition of Anthony Blunt's *Art and Architecture in France 1500-1700* (Harmondsworth, Middlesex, Eng.: Penguin Books, 1981), ill. 239.

[19]For Koch's engraving, see Nassar, p. 53. For Raphael's painting, see almost any survey of his career or of Renaissance art, such as the fourth edition of Frederick Hartt's *History of Italian Renaissance Art: Painting, Sculpture, Architecture* (New York: Harry N. Abrams, 1994), fig. 519.

[20]See Giorgio Vasari's biography of Raphael in *Le vite de' piu eccellenti pittori, scultori ed architettori scritte da Giorgio Vasari*, ed. Gaetano Milanesi, 9 vols. (Florence: Sansoni, 1885-1906).

[21]For more on Ademolli and his work, see A. Renzi, G. Marini, et al., ed. *La "Divina Commedia" di Dante Alighieri con tavole in rame*, 4 vols. (Florence: Tipografia all'insegna dell'Ancora, 1817); A. Ademollo, *Gli spettacoli dell'antica Roma* (Florence: Tipografia all'insegna dell'Ancora, 1837); Luigi Ademolli, *Catalogo delle tavole incise ad acquaforte da Luigi Ademolli* (Florence: Tipografia all'insegna dell'Ancora, 1837); Volkmann; Ulrich Thieme and Feliz Becker, *Allgemeines Lexikon der Bildenden Künstler* (Leipzig: W. Engelmann, 1907-50); Ugo Galletti and Ettora Camesasca, *Enciclopedia della pittura italiana* (Milan: Garzanti, 1951); Emilio Lavagnino, *L'arte moderna dai neoclassici ai contemporanei*, 2 vols. (Turin: Unione tipografico editrice torinese, 1956), I, 260; P. Bucarelli, "Luigi Ademolli," in *Dizionario biografico degli Italiani*, ed. Alberto Maria Ghisalberti (Rome: Istituto della Enciclopedia Italiana, 1960); the entry for Ademolli in the *Enciclopedia dantesca*; and Nassar.

[22]For Ademolli's engraving, see Nassar, p. 287.

[23]For the reference to Cacus running away, see *Inferno* 25.34, and for the quote regarding the dragon, see *Inferno* 25.24.

[24]For the *Laocoön*, see almost any survey of Western art, including *Gardner's Art through the Ages*, fig. 5-89.

[25]For Koch's illustration, see Nassar, p. 291.

[26]Mimesis has, of course, received a great deal of attention in art history and other areas of cultural studies. For a fundamental introduction to it as a topic of the humanities, see Erich Auerbach, *Mimesis: The Representation of Reality in Western Literature* (Princeton: Princeton UP, 1953; repr. 2003). For a fairly extensive, recent bibliography on the topic in general, see Thomas Metscher, *Mimesis* (Bielefeld: Aisthesis, 2001). For recent broad introductions to the relevance of mimesis (and its historiography) for art history, see Gunter Gebauer and Christoph Wulf, *Mimesis: Culture, Art, Society* (Berkeley: University of California Press, 1995); Karol Berger, *A Theory of Art* (New York: Oxford UP, 2000); Robert S. Nelson, ed., *Visuality before and beyond the Renaissance: Seeing as Others Saw* (New York and Cambridge: Cambridge UP, 2000); Stephen Halliwell, *The Aesthetics of Mimesis: Ancient Texts and Modern Problems* (Princeton: Princeton UP, 2002). And

for a fundamental discussion of its duality in art history and elsewhere, see Llowry Nelson, Jr., "The Fictive Reader and Literary Self-Reflexiveness," in *The Disciplines of Criticism: Essays in Literary Theory, Interpretation and History*, ed. Peter Demetz, Thomas Greene, and Lowry Nelson, Jr. (New Haven and London: Yale UP, 1968), 173-91; and, more recently, Andrew E. Benjamin, *Art, Mimesis, and the Avant-Garde: Aspects of a Philosophy of Difference* (New York and London: Routledge, 1991); and Pierre Glaudes, *La représentation dans la littérature et les arts: anthologie* (Toulouse: Presses universitaires du Mirail, 2000).

[27]For more on the role of brush strokes and lines in literally and figuratively foregrounding artists, begin with the work of David Rosand, particularly his latest word on the subject, *Drawing Acts: Studies in Graphic Expression and Representation* (New York: Cambridge UP, 2002).

[28]For Vasari's claim, see his biography of Giotto in *Le vite . . . .* For Botticelli's illustration, see the lower image on page 286 in Nassar.

[29]For Scaramuzza's first publication of his illustrations, see the three-volume edition of the *Commedia* published at Parma in 1865 by A. Saccani and photographed by Carlo Saccani. For other early publications of the illustrations, see *Dante la "divina commedia,"* ed. Giorgio Simona, 4 vols. (Lucerne: Giorgio Simona, n.d.); and *I disegni di Francesco Scaramuzza illustrativi della "Divina commedia"* (Parma: Gazetta de Parma, 1872). For more on Scaramuzza and his work, see Giuseppe Ferrazzi, *Manuale Dantesca* (Bassano: Sante Pozzato, 1865-77); Giovanni A. Scartazzini, "Scaramuzza's Illustrationen zur *Divina Commedia,"* *Allgemeine Zeitung* CCII (1876); Kraus; Volkmann; Giuliano Mambelli, *Gli annali delle edizioni Dantesche* (Bologna: Nicola Zanichelli, 1931); Gianni Capelli and Enrico Dall'Olio, *Francesco Scaramuzza* (Parma: L. Battei, 1974); the entry for Scaramuzza in the *Enciclopedia Dantesca*; Nassar; and Corrado Gizzi, *Francesco Scaramuzza e Dante* (Milan: Electa, 1996).

[30]For Scaramuzza's illustration, see Nassar, p. 70. For the *Expulsion of Heliodorus*, see Hartt, fig. 525.

[31]For *Bacchus and Ariadne*, see Hartt, fig. 622.

[32]Note that, although the concept of decorum was treated by Horace and other ancient critics as a trait to be valued above all in adhering to the proper spirit of dramatic genres and in handling other comparably broad literary issues, it was also welcomed by them, and to an even greater degree by neo-classical critics, in dealing with more minor concerns, such as consistency in the definition of a figure's age and character.

[33]On the relationship(s) between perceived verisimilitude and viewer engagement, see note 12, above.

[34]Ocular dialogues between the viewer and one or more figures have been addressed in numerous studies and assumed in many more. An excellent starting point is still Aloïs Riegl's work, most notably, "Das Hollàndische Gruppenporträt," *Jahrbuch der Kunsthistorischen Sammlungen des Allerhöchsten Kaiserhauses* XXIII (1902), 71-278, excerpts of which have been translated into English and annotated by Benjamin Binstock in *October* LXXIV (Fall 1995), 3-35. See also Jacques Lacan's famous essay "Of the Gaze as *Objet Petit a,"* in *The Four Fundamental Concepts of Psycho-Analysis*, ed. Jacques-Alain Miller, trans. Alan Sheridan (1973; trans. New York: Norton, 1981), 67-119; and Kaja Silverman's brilliant application of it in "Fassbinder and Lacan: A Reconsideration of Gaze, Look and Image," *Camera Obscura* XIX (1989), 54-85.

Remus Lupin and Community:
The Werewolf Tradition in J. K. Rowling's *Harry Potter* Series[1]

Renee Ward

In *Harry Potter and the Prisoner of Azkaban*, J. K. Rowling describes the Dursley family's attitude towards magic as "very medieval" (2-3), a description that Jack Zipes argues "misinterprets history" and reveals Rowling's mediocrity as a writer (178). However, Zipes's criticism overlooks Rowling's acute awareness and manipulation of the sources that inform her work, specifically the lai "Bisclavret" by Marie de France and the Ovidian tale "Lycaon," to which it alludes.[2] Two recent articles co-written by Heather Arden and Kathryn Lorenz establish Rowling's indebtedness to the medieval romance tradition, and to Marie de France, through their discussion of Harry's "outsider" status within the series. Harry, Arden and Lorenz suggest, is a modern day parallel to the French medieval romance heroes Guigemar and Perceval, who are, through their status as heroes, social outsiders.[3]

Through its focus on shape-shifting, this paper similarly emphasizes the connection between medieval romance and the *Harry Potter* series. While all the novels of the series thus far include shape-shifting in some manner, *The Prisoner of Azkaban* centralizes the motif through its Animagi characters, Sirius Black, James Potter, and Peter Pettigrew, and its werewolf figure, Remus Lupin. The following discussion of Rowling's rewriting of the traditional archetypes of the werewolf and the black dog (or the Grim) focuses primarily on the werewolf because of its position, both in literature and history, as a figure repeatedly ostracized by human communities, and unravels how Rowling undermines the outsider status of the werewolf. Rowling's rewriting of the werewolf archetype blurs the boundaries between the werewolf and the black dog, and simultaneously challenges their literary and folkloric antecedents through an associated construction of interlaced communities. These communities not only provide a space within which the werewolf figure occupies an insider status, but they are also inextricably linked to Harry's insider-outsider status, his understanding of hierarchical divisions based on difference, and his developing sense of identity.

In literature, two main werewolf traditions exist: the feral tradition, which reaches back to Ovid and other classical sources, and the sympathetic tradition epitomized by Marie de France.[4] The feral archetype, based on Ovid's Lycaon, is "[f]erocious, hairy, dripping with blood, a devourer of human beings," what Caroline Walker Bynum describes as "an emblem of the periodic eruption of the bestial from within the human" (94). Walker Bynum explains that the feral werewolf is associated with murder and rabid madness, and transgresses the boundaries between humans, and between humans and other species, by committing "the ultimate metamorphosis" of cannibalism, where a human being turns "another person not just into food but into him [or her-] self" (169). This werewolf archetype often appears as a scapegoat in literature. In Ovid's "Lycaon," for example, the transgressions of the king, who mocks the gods and attempts to engage Jove in cannibalism, result not only in his transformation and exile, but also in the destruction of the human race. Jove, distraught by the rebelliousness of humankind embodied in Lycaon, declares that the human race is a cancer, and "cuncta prius temptanda, sed immedicabile curae / ense recidendum, ne pars sincera trahatur" (1.190-91) ["All means should first be tried, but what responds not to the treatment must be cut away with the knife, lest the untainted part also draw infection" (15)].[5] Subsequently, the god destroys the human race by flooding the earth. Thus, Lycaon's behaviour triggers Jove's revenge, and his lupine figure becomes the nexus for the sins of all, resulting in the demise of his nation and the entire human race.

The feral werewolf tradition epitomized by Lycaon had significant sociological impact. During the witch trials of the sixteenth and seventeenth centuries, boundaries blurred between the literary and sociological, as men and women who suffered from the disease of lycanthropy were tried and condemned as werewolves. Lycanthropy often includes dementia, a condition that led many in the late medieval and early modern periods to confess that they were indeed werewolves and were guilty of murder and cannibalism, especially the murder and cannibalism of children. W.M.S. Russell and Clair Russell describe the lycanthrope's physical symptoms as "a tendency to wander about at night, a yellow complexion, hairy skin covered with sores, red teeth, [and] frightening facial deformities" (171). This list of symptoms survives from classical literary werewolves such as Lycaon, whom Ovid describes as a howling, rabid beast with bristling grey hair and gleaming, violent eyes.[6] The exteriority of these symptoms, coupled with the disease's dementia, renders the sufferer a visible "other" to be ostracized and outlawed. In a world where "identity is most clearly defined by difference, that is by what it is not" (Woodward 9), the werewolf, both in literature and society, is condemned and cast out for behavioural and physical difference.

Yet, not all werewolf representations follow this pattern. The medieval romance genre, particularly French medieval romances such as Marie de France's "Bisclavret," develops the "sympathetic" werewolf, a character that transforms but retains "the intelligence and memory" of a rational being (Walker Bynum 74-75). In Marie's tale, the knight and werewolf Bisclavret retains his human rationality despite transformation. Trapped in wolf form by his wife's betrayal, Bisclavret roams the woods for a year, until one day, he sees his feudal lord.

When Bisclavret sees the king, he approaches his side and licks or kisses his stirrups in fealty. Amazed, the king cries out to his companions:

> "Seignur", fet il, "avant venez
> e ceste merveille esguardez,
> cum ceste beste s'umilie!
> Ele a sen d'ume, merci crie.
>
> Chaciez mei tuz cez chiens ariere,
> si guardez que hum ne la fiere!
> Ceste beste a entente e sen.
> Espleitiez vus! Alum nus en!
> A la beste durrai ma pes:
> kar jeo ne chacerai hui mes."
>   (l.151-60)[7]
> "My lords," he said, "come quickly!
> Look at this marvel-
> this beast is humbling itself to me.
> It has the mind of a man, and it's begging me for mercy!
> Chase the dogs away,
> and make sure no one strikes it.
> This beast is rational--he has a mind.
> Hurry up: let's get out of here.
> I'll extend my peace to the creature;
> indeed, I'll hunt no more today!"
>   (Hanning and Ferrante 96)

Because Bisclavret retains his human *sens*, his rationality, while in his wolf form, he recognizes his lord, behaves appropriately, and is ultimately restored to both his human form and appropriate position in society.

The distinction between the feral and the sympathetic werewolf is vital to our understanding of Rowling's depictions of Remus Lupin and Sirius Black. Lupin's physical appearance gestures towards his identity when Harry, Ron, and Hermione first meet him on the train. In *Azkaban*, he wears "an extremely shabby set of wizard's robes" and looks "ill and exhausted" (59); he disappears briefly with each full moon, and, as Hermione correctly guesses, the Boggart becomes a full moon when it faces him. Lupin's tattered and emaciated appearance also indicates his poverty stricken and marginal subsistence, a condition that worsens when he resigns from his post at Hogwarts at the close of *Azkaban*. As we learn in *Order of the Phoenix*, Lupin is unable to procure employment elsewhere because of a piece of "anti-werewolf legislation" drafted by Dolores Umbridge around the time he is employed as the Defence Against the Dark Arts instructor (271). Umbridge's ability to draft and successfully pass such a piece of legislation reflects the wizarding world's view of werewolves as more beast than human, as "savage, four-legged beasts of murderous intent and no human conscience" (*Beasts* x).[8]

Lupin's account of his transformation, like his tattered and emaciated physical appearance, aligns him with the negative image of the werewolf depicted in Newt Scamander's *Fantastic Beasts and Where to Find Them*, which emphasizes, "Almost uniquely among fantastic creatures, the werewolf actively seeks humans in preference to any other kind of prey" (42). Referring to his years as a student at Hogwarts, Lupin explains to Harry, "I became a fully fledged monster once a month," and "[m]y transformations in those days – were terrible. It is very painful to turn into a werewolf. I was separated from humans to bite, so I bit and scratched myself instead" (*Azkaban* 258-59). Lupin's cyclic transformations from human to wolf demonstrate the "eruption of the bestial within the human," outlined by Walker Bynum, and align his transformed self closely to the tradition of the feral, or Ovidian, werewolf (94).

However, while Rowling's werewolf displays the eruptive bestial nature of Ovid's Lycaon, it is, simultaneously, dissimilar. Remus Lupin's human self is not portrayed as consistent with his werewolf form, and Rowling emphasizes this distinction. In Ovid, Lycaon the human is a tyrannical king "notus feritate" (1.198) ["well known for savagery" (17)], a savagery revealed by his cannibalism and defiance of the gods. When Jove transforms Lycaon into a wolf, he only externalizes Lycaon's inner being. Furthermore, Lycaon bears a resemblance to his human form when transformed into wolf form, and,

> cupidine caedis vertitur in pecudes et nunc quoque sanguine gaudet.
> in villos abeunt vestes, in crura lacerti: fit lupus et veteris servat vestigia
> formae; canities eadem est, eadem violentia vultus, idem oculi lucent,
> eadem feritatis imago est. (1.234-39)
> with his accustomed greed for blood he turns against the sheep,
>   delighting
> still in slaughter. His garments change to shaggy hair, his arms to legs. He
> turns into a wolf, and yet retains some traces of his former shape. There is
> the same grey hair, the same fierce face, the same gleaming eyes, the
>   same
> picture of beastly savagery. (19)

Before and after metamorphosis, Lycaon is a ferocious, bloodthirsty being.

Although Lupin is a werewolf, while in human form he is not depicted as mad or insane, as a feral werewolf. As a human, he is much closer to the sympathetic werewolf, which remains, when transformed, a rational being, and throughout *Azkaban* and *Phoenix*, Rowling establishes Lupin's rational and pragmatic behaviour. For example, unlike many of the Hogwarts' professors, Lupin remains unaffected by the poltergeist Peeves, and when insulted by him, responds in a calm, almost amused manner (*Azkaban* 99-100).[9] Further, most of the Hogwarts' instructors respect Lupin, even Madam Pomfrey, who declares with approval that he "knows his remedies" (70) because he gave Harry and his friends chocolate after their first encounter with a Dementor. Lupin demonstrates his clearheaded and thoughtful nature through his position as a Hogwarts instructor, and, especially, through his role as a mediator. When Professor Snape insults Neville Longbottom's skill in front of the entire Defence Against the Dark Arts class and other teachers, Lupin counters the insult and restores (somewhat) Neville's dignity by informing Snape, "I was hoping that Neville would assist me with the first stage of the operation, ... and I am sure he will perform it admirably" (100).

The diffusion of tense situations is, indeed, Lupin's specialty. When members of the secret society, the Order of the Phoenix, particularly Sirius Black and Molly Weasley, are at loggerheads about how much information Harry should receive about the activities of Voldemort and his followers, the activities of the Order itself, and Harry's role in both, it is Lupin who restores peace and resolves the debate. He suggests that it is better for Harry to receive accurate but general information from the Order "rather than a garbled version from...others," demonstrating his awareness that, even if excluded from the meetings, Harry, Hermione, and the Weasley children would eavesdrop anyway (*Phoenix* 85).[10] Much of Lupin's behaviour suggests that he has the best interests of others, particularly of Harry, foremost in mind. He covers for Harry and Ron when they are in trouble with Snape, and his presence curbs Malfoy's behaviour on numerous occasions. More importantly, Lupin reminds Harry that he cannot "cover" for him all the time; Harry needs to behave in a more responsible manner in order to avoid difficult situations (*Azkaban* 213). Lupin also provides Harry with private tutelage, teaching him the Patronus charm that ultimately saves Harry and Sirius's lives. As Owen Dudley Edwards suggests, Lupin perpetuates "the tradition of the hero finding fosterage or pupilage among convenient animals or hybrids, a role the centaurs, especially Chiron, undertook for sundry Greek heroes, or the wolf who nursed Romulus and Remus" undertook for the twin founders of Rome (115).[11] Lupin, Edwards argues, combines the centaur-tutor and wolf-guardian figures through his name, Remus Lupin, his identity as a werewolf, and his status as the professor of Defence Against the Dark Arts (115). Lupin, then, is both feral and sympathetic werewolf, as well as the animal or beast tutor figure of classical myth.

Like Remus Lupin, Sirius Black is not what he appears. In the opening chapters of *Azkaban*, Black's description identifies him, more so than Lupin, with the feral werewolf. He first appears on the news as a "gaunt face...surrounded by a matted, elbow-length tangle" of hair (18), an image repeated when he appears in the *Daily Prophet* as "a sunken-faced man with long, matted hair" (33). When Harry sees a photo in the newspaper, he cannot help but notice the vampire-like quality of Black's "shadowed eyes," "sunken face," and "waxy white skin" (34). According to the Cornelius Fudge, the Minister for Magic, Black is *"mad"* and *"a danger to anyone who crosses him"* (33), a deranged criminal responsible for the murder of his best friends and the slaughter of innocent people. Although Rowling portrays Black as an insane mass-murderer with a lycanthropic physicality, as a literal depiction of the feral werewolf archetype, she later reveals that he is, in fact, an Animagus, and therefore closer to the sympathetic werewolf because he retains his human *sens* during metamorphosis. This revelation, however, does not initially render Black any less bloodthirsty or ferocious than the previous descriptions of him. Despite the ability to retain his human rationality, Black appears to possess very little in either form. When Harry, Ron, and Hermione meet Black as a human in the Shrieking Shack, he is consumed by the desire to kill Ron's pet rat Scabbers, who we learn is actually the Animagus Peter Pettigrew. Black struggles against Lupin's restraint, lunging after Scabbers/Peter, and relents only when Lupin pleads with him that Harry needs to know the truth. Even then, Black says, "make it quick, Remus. I want to commit the murder I was imprisoned for" (256-57). He watches the rat "with a horrible sort of hunger in his face" (260), and when he speaks, his words come out in a "snarl" (260) or "growl" (270). In human form, Black appears far more ferocious than Lupin. Indeed, it is Lupin (once again in his mediator role) who remains calm, restrains Black, and insists that the situation be explained fully to Harry before any actions occur.

While Rowling blurs the werewolf archetypes through her descriptions of Lupin and Black, she finally confirms Black's identity as the black dog (the Grim), another archetype with an extensive background and dual identity, one found primarily in folklore. Harry usually sees the Grim, or "the hulking outline of something very big, with wide, gleaming eyes" (30), at night, in shadows, in laneways, or on the edge of the Forbidden Forest. Associated with liminal spaces such as crossroads, gateways, hollow trees, and other places considered "passages downwards to the World of the Dead," the Grim is often interpreted as a harbinger of death (Brown 47). Black's supposed murder of the Potters and of other innocent people aligns him with this interpretation. However, as Theo Brown points out, the Grim is also frequently interpreted as a protector figure or as a warning sign, one that "only manifests itself visually at times of crisis – death, danger, illness" (53). The difference between these roles of protector and harbinger of death lies solely in one's interpretation, and Black embodies, at different stages of the text, both identities. Throughout most of the novel, Harry believes the Grim haunts him as the portent of death;

ultimately, however, Sirius reveals that he, like Lupin, is a protector figure. Furthermore, we discover, along with Harry, Ron, and Hermione, that Black is innocent of the murders for which he was sent to Azkaban. Black's actual target throughout the book is the real murderer, Scabbers/Peter Pettigrew. Only a misinterpretation by both Harry and Professor Trelawney aligns the black dog with Harry's "impending" death, not any actions pursued by the Grim itself: Sirius Black never truly portends death for Harry.[12]

Rowling's text differs from other werewolf narratives because it combines the sympathetic and feral werewolf tales not only with each other but also with the folkloric tradition of the Grim. Furthermore, through the figures of the werewolf and the Grim, Rowling creates a number of interlaced communities in which Lupin, the ostracized werewolf, finds social acceptance. In doing so, Rowling rejects the exiled werewolf of Ovid and instead follows the tradition epitomized by Marie de France of the sympathetic werewolf who is restored to society. Moreover, Rowling surrounds her werewolf with like-minded characters who, like Lupin, transgress the species boundary. While students at Hogwarts, James Potter, Sirius Black, and Peter Pettigrew train themselves in Transfiguration and become Animagi in order to accompany Lupin when he is in his transformed state. These Animagi companions, in their transformed states, have a calming effect on Lupin. "My body was still wolfish," he says, "but my mind seemed to become less so while I was with them" (*Azkaban* 260). Thus, while Lupin remains the werewolf figure that lacks *sens*, this differential is significantly reduced when the Animagi surround him. It is also important to remember here that Lupin's companions are, ultimately, human. Although James, Sirius, and Peter transform to keep Lupin company, they are sympathetic wer-creatures; whether stag, dog, or rat, they all retain their human self while in animal form. The Animagi's transgressions are therefore doubled because they develop their abilities in Transfiguration outside of the strictures of the classroom and remain unregistered Animagi. They risk persecution to create a community within which the werewolf belongs, and through their transgression of the Ministry's regulations, themselves become outlaws.

Lupin's return to Hogwarts results in his reunion with Black, and the development of new friendships with Harry, Ron, and Hermione. The partial restoration of Lupin's previous community at Hogwarts echoes the tradition of the sympathetic werewolf Bisclavret, who, although restored to society, experiences a reduced society through the removal of his disloyal wife. However, Lupin's new friendships, especially the tutor-guardian relationship Lupin has with Harry, and his involvement in the original and reformed Order of the Phoenix, differentiate him from his literary antecedents. Lupin's community/communities continually expand and intertwine as the *Harry Potter* series progresses, distancing him from the feral werewolf archetype with which the wizarding community at large associates him and undermining his status as a social outsider. Rowling's narrative embraces the werewolf figure beyond even the precedent set by sympathetic werewolf narratives such as "Bisclavret."

Lupin's position within the series is also a central one because his relationship with Harry is intrinsic to Harry's development. During *Azkaban*, Harry encounters his own capacity for anger and hate. After his visit to Hogsmeade and the discovery that Black betrayed his parents, Harry returns to his dormitory and examines his photo album. It has a profound effect, and "[a] hatred such as he had never known before" courses through him "like poison" (158). While Harry has previously experienced anger, indeed has been angry enough to torment his cousin, to attack Malfoy, or to blow up Aunt Marge, he has never expressed such hatred. These emotions escalate when Harry meets Black in the Shrieking Shack:

> A boiling hate erupted in Harry's chest, leaving no place for fear. For the first time in his life, he wanted his wand back in his hand, not to defend himself, but to attack... to kill.
>
> [. . . . .]
>
> All Harry knew was that he wanted to hurt Black as badly as he could and he didn't care how much he got hurt in return. (249)

In this moment, evil and black emotions erupt from Harry's chest just as the bestial erupts from the human during a werewolf's transformation. Harry becomes, briefly, the being without human reason and is consumed by his desire to kill. He is, in this instance, both feral werewolf and Grim: bloodthirsty beast and harbinger of death.

Harry's relationship with and to Lupin alters our understanding of the werewolf as a socially ostracized figure. Despite witnessing Lupin's transformation into a ferocious werewolf (*Azkaban* 278-79), Harry still wants him to remain the Defence Against the Dark Arts teacher. When Lupin explains how Snape "let it slip" that he was a werewolf, Harry exclaims, "You're not leaving just because of that!" (309). Harry's witnessing of Lupin's transformation, a feature that sets Rowling's werewolf narrative apart from her sources,[13] solidifies the bond between pupil and tutor and enables Harry to recognize that, despite what one's physical being or innermost self may be capable of, one's choices ultimately constitute one's identity. Harry sees beyond Lupin's outcast werewolf status and, rather than reducing his character to a single, feral essence, recognizes the complexity of identity and the many manifestations that it can take. Harry's introduction to Black, followed by the revelation of truth, reinforces the lessons he learns through Lupin: that appearances are not always indicative of a person's nature, that the capacity for darkness does not determine the entire nature of a being, and, finally, that the persecution of others based upon such criteria is ultimately unjust.

Harry's communities, like Lupin's, expand throughout the series to include surrogate families with the Weasleys, Hagrid, and Dumbledore, and, in *Azkaban*, a surrogate family with Lupin and a primary family with his godfather Sirius Black; a peer group within Gryffindor; "companions of the heart" with Ron and Hermione;[14] and a sport group through his position as Seeker on the Gryffindor Quidditch team. Despite his status as an orphan and the fame he experiences as "The Boy Who Lived," both of which isolate or set him apart from others, Harry, as the hero, experiences an unusually large number of human communities. This feature distances him from Guigemar and Perceval, the French medieval romance heroes that Arden and Lorenz align him with, who have limited human contact. More notably, this feature distances Harry from other youth's fantasy literature heroes such as T. H. White's Wart (*The Sword in the Stone*) or Ursula K. LeGuin's Ged (*A Wizard of Earthsea*), both of whom experience and require a decrease in human interaction as their exposure to shape-shifting increases.[15] Indeed, in these examples, separation or isolation allows the hero to develop the skills necessary to complete his ultimate task or challenge. In contrast, Rowling emphasizes the need for her protagonist to be immersed in a human-based community in order to succeed.

The importance of Harry's human relationships and their impact on his development becomes increasingly clear in *Order of the Phoenix*. Besides Lupin and Black, others such as Ron (with his interest in sports) and Hermione (with her prudence and 'book' smarts) contribute to Harry's development and, more importantly, to his success against Voldemort. In the first book of the series, the skills of Ron and Hermione are essential to Harry's success and allow him to pass through the barriers protecting the Philosopher's Stone.[16] In *Phoenix*, Ron's status at Hogwarts significantly changes when he joins the Gryffindor Quidditch team. Ron's exposure to the negative criticism and scrutiny associated with his initial lack of success as Keeper for the team echoes the attention Harry has received since his arrival at Hogwarts, much of which is also negative. Ron, who has always been somewhat jealous of the attention Harry receives, gains insight to the positive and negative aspects of always being the centre of attention, which will ultimately inform his understanding of his friend and his friend's position in the wizarding world.[17] Hermione's prudence serves as a cautionary measure, and even though she argues that Harry's vision of Sirius could be a trap, "Harry recognises [her] offer to accompany him into Umbridge's office as a sign of solidarity and loyalty" (650).

When Umbridge, at the behest of the Ministry of Magic, restricts the Defense Against the Dark Arts curriculum to theoretical material only, Hermione suggests to Harry that he provide for herself and others practical instruction that will not only prepare them for their Ordinary Wizarding Level exams, but also for attacks from Voldemort and his followers. The group that they form, the group that coins itself Dumbledore's Army (DA), is a microcosm of the Order of the Phoenix. Not only does it provide a space within which underage wizards may actively resist the Ministry's denial of Voldemort's return, but it also has a leveling effect on the society at Hogwarts and unites most of the school in a way that the Sorting Hat suggested at the start of year.[18] Dumbledore's Army includes members from three of the four Hogwarts houses: Gryffindor, Hufflepuff, and Ravenclaw. Only Slytherin members remain uninvolved. The creation of Dumbledore's Army also provides Harry with significant experience as a leader and teacher, as he instructs and reinforces the confidence of his pupils. Even Neville Longbottom, famous for his ineptitude with most subjects, does well during the DA meetings, and it is Neville who reminds Harry that he is not alone in his efforts to resist Voldemort. When Harry wants to rush to the Ministry to save Sirius, Neville reminds him,

> 'We were all in the DA together,' said Neville quietly. 'It was all supposed to be about fighting You-Know-Who, wasn't it? And this is the first chance we've had to do something real – or was that all just a game or something?'

'No – of course it wasn't -' said Harry impatiently.

'Then we should come too,' said Neville simply. 'We want to help.' (671) Strength and success, Neville suggests, lie in their efforts to work together, not alone.

The creation of the DA teaches a similar lesson to, of all people, Professor Dumbledore. Dumbledore, along with a number of others, excludes Harry and his friends from the Order because they believe that, as underage wizards, the students are not yet prepared to face Voldemort and his Death Eaters. Dumbledore, one of Harry's most crucial surrogate familial figures, notably distances himself from Harry because he fears Voldemort will use Harry to access him. However, the Order's exclusion of Harry (and his friends), and Dumbledore's limiting of Harry's knowledge concerning Voldemort and the Order's activities, backfire. These exclusions are precisely what lead Harry into Voldemort's trap and place his life and the lives of his friends in danger. While we eventually learn that Harry must, ultimately, face Voldemort alone and that one of them will die, Rowling reinforces the need for community at the end of *Phoenix*, and suggests that Harry will only be successful in such a match if supported by a community. When the Hogwarts Express arrives at Platform 9¾, Harry finds "a group of people standing there to greet him who he had not expected at all": Mad-Eye Moody, Tonks, Lupin, Mr. and Mrs. Weasley, and the twins, Fred and George Weasley (764). On the final page, Mad-Eye tells Harry, "give us a shout if you need us," and Lupin reminds him "Keep in touch" (766). In response, Harry nods, and, as Rowling writes, "He somehow could not find words to tell them what it meant to him, to see them all ranged there, *on his side*" (766, emphasis mine).

In her discussion of metamorphosis and identity in medieval and classical narratives, Walker Bynum argues, "we surely need a more labile and problematic understanding of identity" (165-66). Rowling provides exactly what Walker Bynum desires. In *Harry Potter and the Prisoner of Azkaban*, she complicates concepts of identity through her rewriting of the werewolf figure. Rowling's werewolf, Remus Lupin, is a complex blend not only of the traditional werewolf archetypes – of the feral Ovidian werewolf Lycaon and the sympathetic Bisclavret of Marie de France – but also of these traditions with the folkloric figure of the black dog and the tutor figure of classical myth. Rowling's departure from representations of the werewolf as the vilified and ostracized figure reveals that her work is anything but, as Zipes would claim, "conventional and predictable" (175). Moreover, Rowling's strategic relocation of the werewolf during transformation from an unwitnessed to a witnessed forum and her witness-protagonist's subsequent acceptance of the werewolf move beyond even the example of Marie de France's sympathetic werewolf narrative. Rowling's understanding, not her misinterpretation, of medieval (and consequently classical) sources allows her to create a unique werewolf figure, one that reveals her awareness and manipulation of the historical and literary traditions within which she works. Furthermore, Rowling's manipulation of her sources renders Remus Lupin a social insider to a series of interconnected communities of like-minded and often transgressive wizards, both old and young, all of which connect the werewolf to the protagonist and contribute to the protagonist's development. While at the end of *Azkaban* Lupin leaves Hogwarts, this is a short-lived return to outsider status, and as Harry's reaction to Lupin's departure makes clear, it is one based on artificial boundaries designed to keep those with differences, particularly physical differences, outside of society. Lupin's reappearance in *Order of the Phoenix* places him alongside Harry, and firmly within a community that will become the ultimate "insider society" within the wizarding world through its eventual defeat of Voldemort.

UNIVERSITY OF ALBERTA

NOTES

[1] A shorter version of this paper, titled "Remus Lupin and the Werewolf Tradition: *Harry Potter and the Prisoner of Azkaban*," was presented on 1 October 2004 at the *Nineteenth*

Annual Meeting of the International Conference on Medievalism, University of New Brunswick, Fredericton, NB, Canada.

[2] This paper focuses on Ovid's werewolf narrative rather than other classical tales because of Ovid's preeminence as a classical source in the medieval period, and, more importantly, because Marie de France "evinces an awareness of borrowing from the past" in her General Prologue the *Lais* (Gertz 99). Despite Marie's choice to write tales based on Breton lais, her tales still create a dialogue with the classical Latin sources that she rejects. See SunHee Kim Gertz, "Transforming Lovers and Memorials in Ovid and Marie de France," *Florilegium* 14 (1995): 99-122. Marie de France states in her Prologue, "Pur ceo començai a penser / d'alkune bone estoire faire / e de Latin en Romanz traire; / mais ne me fust guaires de pris: / itant s'en sunt altre entremis" (l. 28-32) [Voilà pourquoi j'ai d'abord eu l'idée / de composer un bon récit / que j'aurais traduit de latin en français. Mais je n'en aurais pas tiré grande estime / car tant d'autres l'ont déjà fait!] ["That's why I began to think / about composing some good stories / and translating from Latin to Romance; / but that was not to bring me fame: / too many others have done it" (28-29).] All French quotations are from *Lais de Marie de France*, trans. Laurence Harf-Lancner, ed. Karl Warnke (Paris: Librairie Générale Française, 1990). All in-text citations are from Warnke's edition of the Old French, while Harf-Lancner's modern French translation is provided in the endnotes. All French citations include a corresponding English translation from *The Lais of Marie de France*, trans. Robert Hanning and Joan Ferrante (Grand Rapids: BakerBooks, 1978). Line references for all French citations are the same; all English translation citations indicate page number.

[3] Heather Arden and Kathryn Lorenz, "The Ambiguity of the Outsider in the Harry Potter Series and Beyond," *The Image of the Outsider in Literature, Media and Society*, ed. Will Wright and Steven Kaplan (Pueblo, CO: Society for the Interdisciplinary Study of Social Imagery, University of Southern Colorado, 2002) 430-34, and "The Harry Potter Stories and French Arthurian Romance," *Arthuriana* 13.2 (Summer 2003): 54-68.

[4] Some other popular classical werewolf narratives include versions of the Lycaon tale by Pausanias and Apollodorus, Vergil's character 'Moeris' in his *Eclogues* (c. 48-32 B.C.E.), and the tale of Trimalchio's Banquet in Petronius' *Satyricon* (c. 1 C.E.). Other medieval narratives include Gerald of Wales' *Topographia Hibernia* (2.19), Gervase of Tilbury's *Otia Imperialia* (3.120), the lai of Mélion, and *Guillaume de Palerne*, a French romance. For discussions on these tales, see, for example, Joyce E. Salisbury, *The Beast Within: Animals in the Middle Ages* (New York and London: Routledge, 1994); Kirby F. Smith, "An Historical Study of the Werewolf in Literature," *Publications of the Modern Language Association of America* n.s. 2.1 [9.1] (1984): 1-42; or Caroline Walker Bynum, *Metamorphosis and Identity* (New York: Zone Books, 2001).

[5] All Latin and English citations are from Ovid, *Metamorphoses*, trans. Frank Justice Miller, vol. 1 of 2 (Cambridge, MA: Harvard University Press, 1977). Latin citations use line numbers, while the English translation, which does not list line numbers, uses page numbers.

[6] Lycaon "exululat frustraque loqui conatur" (l.238-39) ["howls aloud, attempting in vain to speak"; l.232], and in his appearance "canities eadem est, eadem violentia vultus, / idem oculi lucent" [There is the same grey hair, the same fierce face, the same gleaming eyes" (19)].

[7] "'Seigneurs, venez donc / voir ce prodige, / voyez comme cette bête se prosterne! / Elle a l'intelligence d'un homme, elle implore ma grâce. / Faites-moi reculer tous ces chiens / et que nul la touche! / Cette bête est douée de raison et d'intelligence! Dépechez-vous; allons-nous-en! / J'accorde ma protection à cette bête / et j'arrête la chasse pour aujourd'hui!'" (l.151-60).

[8] Newt Scamander [J. K. Rowling] briefly recounts the difficulty the Ministry of Magic has with its classification of the werewolf, indeed, with the overall definitions of what constitutes a "beast" or a "being." The current definitions were introduced in 1811 by the then Minister for Magic, Grogan Stump, who declared, "a 'being' was 'any creature that has sufficient intelligence to understand the laws of the magical community and to bear part of the responsibility in shaping those laws'" (xii). Scamander goes on to explain that werewolves "have been shunted between the Beast and Being divisions for many years; at the time of writing there is an office for Werewolf Support Services at the Being Division whereas the Werewolf Registry and Werewolf Capture Unit fall under the Beast Division" (xiii). See Newt Scamander, *Fantastic Beasts and Where to Find Them* (Vancouver: Raincoast Books, 2001).

[9] I am grateful to Dr. Andrea Schutz for sharing her upcoming conference paper with me in advance, and for reminding me of this point by doing so. Andrea's paper, "Beings and the Beast," focuses on Remus Lupin's status within the wizarding world and will be presented at the University of Reading, England, *Accio 2005*, Harry Potter Conference.

[10] We learn in *Order of the Phoenix* that Lupin also held a mediator type role as a Prefect while a student at Hogwarts. Sirius tells Harry that Lupin was "a good boy," while Lupin speculates that Dumbledore made him a Prefect with the hope that he "would be able to exercise some control" over his trouble-making friends, James and Sirius (155).

[11] Rowling plays upon this tradition even earlier, in *The Philosopher's Stone*, when the centaur Firenze rescues Harry Potter from Voldemort, whom Harry stumbles across feasting on the blood of a dead unicorn. Firenze also acts, in this instance, as a tutor figure, when he tells Harry, "The blood of a unicorn will keep you alive, even if you are an inch from death, but at a terrible price. You have slain something pure and defenceless to save yourself and you will have but a half life, a cursed life, from the moment the blood touches your lips" (*Philosopher's Stone* 188). Firenze also appears in a similar position when, near the end of *Phoenix*, Dumbledore appoints him as the new Divination teacher (527).

[12] Of course, as the Grim, Sirius Black does portend death for Peter Pettigrew, and, ironically, Sirius himself finds death in a later volume when he tries to protect Harry, is struck by a spell from Bellatrix Lestrange, and then falls through the veil. See *Phoenix*, 710-11. It is worthwhile to note, also, that Sirius Black's death is the subject of much speculation amongst readers on fan-based internet sources. Any web search on the topic will reveal countless chat rooms and notice boards where the consensus is that Sirius is not truly dead. See, for example, Amenuensis1, "The Not-So-Certain Death of Sirius Black," online posting, 24 May 2004, livejournal.com, 4 January 2005, http://www.livejournal.com/users/amanuensis1/64862.html; the "Remembering Sirius Memorial Book" at *Lightning Scar*, 12 May 2004, Lisa Web Design Studios, 4 January

2005, http://littlemisswebmaster.co.uk; or the web site *Black Isn't Dead*, 27 December 2004, 4 January 2005, http://www.poetic-genius.org/black/index2.html.

[13] Walker Bynum points out that Bisclavret's metamorphoses remain "undescribed" or unwitnessed throughout the lai (173). Indeed, Bisclavret refuses to transform in the public space of the court and only does so within the privacy of "la chambre" (l.297) ["the king's chamber" (100)]. Similarly, Lycaon's transformation is described for the reader but is unwitnessed within the text, as he flees to "silentia ruris" (l.232) ["the silent fields" (19)] prior to transformation.

[14] Mary Pharr uses this term to describe companions who "let the hero laugh and feel a normalcy otherwise denied" (62). Pharr aligns Harry with heroes such as Gilgamesh or Luke Skywalker precisely because they all have "companions of the heart," and, she argues, "if the gift of such friendship is allowed the hero, it humanizes him" (62). To emphasize this point, Pharr lists the heroes Beowulf and Arthur among those who lack such friendship and are thus distanced from humanity. While Pharr's discussion concerns Harry, the example of the werewolf and the Animagi in *Harry Potter and the Prisoner of Azkaban* demonstrates how "companions of the heart" can "humanize" figures other than the hero. See Mary Pharr, "In Media Res: Harry Potter as Hero-in-Progress," *The Ivory Tower and Harry Potter: Perspectives on a Literary Phenomenon*, ed. Lana A. Whited (Columbia: University of Missouri Press, 2002), 53-66.

[15] Removal from human community forms part of the "separation" stage in the development of the hero "separation-initiation-return" pattern. See Joseph Campbell, *The Hero With a Thousand Faces*, Bollingen Series 17 (Princeton: Princeton UP, 1968), 30. Arden and Lorenz argue that this pattern of the Campbellian monomyth aligns Harry with his medieval counterparts, Guigemar ("Ambiguity" 430) and Perceval ("Harry Potter Stories" 61).

[16] Chapter Sixteen, "Through the Trapdoor," *Harry Potter and the Philosopher's Stone*.

[17] "The only thing really worrying Harry was how much Ron was allowing the tactics of the Slytherin team to upset him before they even got on the pitch. Harry, of course, had endured their snide comments for over four years, ... But Ron had never endured a relentless campaign of insults, jeers and intimidation" (*Phoenix* 355).

[18] At the opening feast, the Hat sang, "*For our Hogwarts is in danger / From external, deadly foes / And we must unite inside her / Or we'll crumble from within*" (*Phoenix* 186-87).

WORKS CITED

Arden, Heather, and Kathryn Lorenz. "The Ambiguity of the Outsider in the Harry Potter Series and Beyond." *The Image of the Outsider in Literature, Media and Society*. Ed. Will Wright and Steven Kaplan. Pueblo, CO: Society for the Interdisciplinary Study of Social Imagery, University of Southern Colorado, 2002. 430-34.

_____. "The Harry Potter Stories and French Arthurian Romance." *Arthuriana* 13.2 (Summer 2003): 54-68.

Brown, Theo. "The Black Dog in English Folklore." *Animals in Folklore*. Ed. J. R. Porter and W. M. S. Russell. Cambridge: D. S. Brewer, 1978. 45-58.

Campbell, Joseph. *The Hero With a Thousand Faces*. Bollingen Series 17. Princeton: Princeton UP, 1968.

Edwards, Owen Dudley. "Harry Potter and History." *The Chesterton Review* 27.1-2 (Feb-May 2001): 112-19.

Gertz, SunHee Kim. "Transforming Lovers and Memorials in Ovid and Marie de France." *Florilegium* 14 (1995-96): 99-122.

Lais de Marie de France. Trans. Laurence Harf-Lancner. Ed. Karl Warnke. Paris: Librairie Générale Française, 1990.

The Lais of Marie de France. Trans. Robert Hanning and Joan Ferrante. Grand Rapids: BakerBooks, 1978.

LeGuin, Ursula K. *A Wizard of Earthsea*. Berkeley, CA: Parnassus, 1968.

Ovid. *Metamorphoses*. Trans. Frank Justice Miller. Vol. 1 of 2. Cambridge, MA: Harvard UP, 1977.

Pharr, Mary. "In Media Res: Harry Potter as Hero-in-Progress." *The Ivory Tower and Harry Potter: Perspectives on a Literary Phenomenon*. Ed. Lana A. Whited. Columbia: U of Missouri P, 2002. 53-66.

Rowling, J. K. *Harry Potter and the Philosopher's Stone*. London: Bloomsbury, 1997.

_____. *Harry Potter and the Prisoner of Azkaban*. London: Bloomsbury, 1999.

_____. *Harry Potter and the Order of the Phoenix*. London: Bloomsbury, 2003.

Russell, W.M.S. and Clair Russell. "The Social Biology of Werewolves." *Animals in Folklore*. Ed. J.R. Porter and W.M.S. Russell. Cambridge: D. S. Brewer, 1978. 143-82.

Salisbury, Joyce E. *The Beast Within: Animals in the Middle Ages*. New York and London: Routledge, 1994.

Scamander, Newt [J. K. Rowling]. *Fantastic Beasts and Where to Find Them*. Vancouver: Raincoast Books, 2001.

Smith, Kirby F. "An Historical Study of the Werewolf in Literature." *Publications of the Modern Language Association of America* n.s. 2.1 [9.1] (1984): 1-42.

Walker Bynum, Caroline. *Metamorphosis and Identity*. New York: Zone Books, 2001.

White. T. H. *The Sword in the Stone*. London: William Collins Sons, 1938.

Woodward, Kathryn. "Concepts of Identity and Difference." *Identity and Difference*. Ed. Kathryn Woodward. London: Sage, 1997. 8-62.

Zipes, Jack. *Sticks and Stones: The Troublesome Success of Children's Literature from Slovenly Peter to Harry Potter*. New York and London: Routledge, 2001.

Architectural Restoration and Stained Glass in 19th-Century Siena: The Place of Light in Giuseppe Partini's *Purismo*

Nancy M. Thompson

In the decades surrounding the unification of Italy in 1861, many Tuscan artists and intellectuals became increasingly concerned with the resurrection and preservation of their medieval past.[1] In Siena, the architect Giuseppe Partini (1842-95) led a campaign to restore the city's medieval churches and civic buildings as part of this greater movement. Inspired by the ideas of Viollet-le-Duc in France, Partini strove to return Siena's medieval buildings to a state that reflected the ideas of the original architects. While Partini worked on hundreds of projects during his life, he was also continuously occupied with the restoration of the Siena cathedral due to his position as its chief architect. One of his chief concerns was the illumination of the cathedral's interior, because he believed that the proper interior light would inspire Catholic devotion in nineteenth-century visitors. Consequently, during his tenure as architect, all of the clerestory windows were enlarged and equipped with new stained glass, a fifteenth-century window from S. Francesco in Colle Val d'Elsa was restored and installed in the left and right transepts, and new stained glass was made for the windows at the base of the cupola. A great majority of the glass was made or restored by Partini's friend and frequent collaborator Ulisse De Matteis (1827-1910).[2] As a discussion of their collaborative work at the Siena cathedral will demonstrate, the restoration and recreation of medieval stained glass and architecture was also a significant political statement within the context of the Italian liberation and the ideology of *purismo*, which upheld the medieval as the pinnacle of artistic achievement in Tuscany.

Born in 1842, Giuseppe Partini was raised by his parents Bonizella, a seamstress, and Giovanbattista, an engraver, in Via Salicotto in Siena.[3] Despite the reluctance of his parents, Partini entered the architectural academy in Siena in 1857 and studied under Lorenzo Doveri and Giulio Rossi.[4] Following the completion of his studies in 1861, Partini's career grew rapidly: he built a private chapel for the Nerli in the Siena cemetery, submitted a design for the façade of the Florence cathedral, which placed within the top six finalists, built a monument to his former professor Rossi, and directed the project to install a copy of the Fonte Gaia in the Palazzo Pubblico.[5] Following Doveri's death in 1866, Partini moved on to fill his shoes, first as professor of Architecture at the Accademia di Belle Arti in Siena and then, in 1867, as the chief architect of the Siena Cathedral.[6]

Partini was one of many artists who came of age in a Tuscany that fostered the revival of late medieval art. As Tuscany emerged from Austrian rule and

joined the sovereign Kingdom of Italy in 1861, artists and cultural critics came
to consider the Baroque and neo-classical art created in Italy under Medici rule
and subsequent Austrian domination as decadent and in poor taste. In an essay
written in 1847 entitled "Sullo studio de' maestri antichi e sugli ostacoli che ad
esso si frappongono,"[7] Luigi Mussini (1815-88), director of the Istituto di Belle
Arti in Siena from 1851 and the leader of the popular artistic movement called
purismo, charges Tuscan artists to look for inspiration to the period before the
Medici duchy to understand the true nature of art.[8] He laments that, while there
is a great deal of discussion of Raphael, the fourteenth and fifteenth-century
churches of Florence, Santa Trinita, and the Carmine in particular are empty of
Florentines and tourists. When Mussini wrote this essay in 1847, there was very
little interest in reviving the Middle Ages in Tuscany; Mussini was influenced
instead by the German Nazarene movement, whose leaders he had met in
Rome. Mussini advocated a return to the religiosity of the Italian primitives, in
particular Tuscan art of the thirteenth through fifteenth centuries, in order to
create a new Catholic art that would inspire devotion in nineteenth-century
Italians.[9] Mussini's purismo was influential in Florence and Siena in particular:
already in the 1850s, artists in his circle rejected the neo-classical style promoted
by art academies in Italy and France because they associated neo-classicism with
the artistic ideals of the Austrian and Napoleonic regimes that had occupied
Tuscany.[10] In the period following the ousting of the Austrians from Tuscany
in 1859 and the political unification of the Italian peninsula in 1861, the revival
of the medieval signified a return to "true" Italian art, created in a period
when Tuscan artists, motivated by genuine spirituality, practiced their craft in
an environment free from political oppression.[11] The medieval architectural
monuments of Siena were highly significant in this cultural climate, and the
values of the purists motivated Partini to restore the churches of Siena to what
he believed to be their medieval states.

The desire to return to an authentic Tuscan medieval art also inspired
Ulisse De Matteis to revive the art of stained glass in Florence. De Matteis
began his career in stained glass in 1859, when he became the artistic director
of the Francini glass company in Florence. On the first page of a sales catalog
published in 1915, the firm boasts that it creates and restores windows "secondo
il sistema degli antichi maestri."[12] Although this was written five years after
Ulisse De Matteis' death, artists and critics who wrote in the numerous journals
published in Florence during the late nineteenth century consistently praised
his work for its fidelity to the work of the "ancient masters." In a brief article
written in 1870 that details the history of the firm and its commissions, Antonio
Pavan specifically praises De Matteis for the window he made for the façade
of the cathedral in San Minato al Tedesco.[13] Pavan notes that this window
of the Assumption of the Virgin won a medal at the 1861 Italian exhibition

because it so perfectly imitated the *antico*.[14] While the *opera* of San Miniato wanted De Matteis to include the extant fragments of the original window in his restoration, De Matteis deemed them too corroded.[15] For a model for his authentic recreation, De Matteis evidently looked to the *tondo* of the Assumption in the façade of the Florence cathedral designed by Ghiberti and carried out by Niccolò di Piero Tedesco in 1405.[16] The success of the San Miniato window, an important milestone in De Matteis' early career, established his reputation and earned him subsequent commissions in many of the most important buildings in Florence. From the mid 1860s until the end of his career, De Matteis made new windows for Santa Croce and restored the majority of fourteenth and fifteenth-century stained glass in the church. In 1869, the Englishman Francis Sloane purchased the Spinelli chapel just to the right of church's high altar, and as part of the chapel's restoration, Sloane commissioned De Matteis to create a window in a medieval style.[17] The window, praised by Mussini in a speech he delivered to the French Institute in 1870 on Santa Croce's recent restoration, was modeled on the early fourteenth-century window in the Bardi chapel dedicated to the Holy Confessors at the end of the left transept.[18] In the Sloane window, De Matteis recreated the Bardi window's geometric outlines and decorative and vegetal motifs, as well as the figural compositions. In an inscription on the left wall of the chapel, the restorer's goals are made clear: through the 1869 restoration, the chapel was returned to its ancient form by following the traces of the original construction of 1295.[19] In fact, Mussini praises De Matteis and the architectural restorers who worked at Santa Croce for ridding Santa Croce of the bad taste of the later Renaissance and Baroque periods, thereby making a "most admirable monument of the Middle Ages" visible once again.[20] In keeping with Mussini's charge in his 1847 essay, De Matteis looked back to the fourteenth and fifteenth centuries, to the period of "true" Tuscan medieval art, to find inspiration for his new stained glass windows.

The removal of Baroque additions to medieval churches was also of central concern to Partini, as it had been to his mentor Lorenzo Doveri. In the later years of his tenure as architect, Doveri proposed to remove many of the Baroque additions to the Siena Cathedral as part of a larger plan to restore the structure.[21] After some urgent stabilizing of the cathedral's structure damaged in an earthquake, Doveri recommended first cleaning and then repairing and organizing the interior. In the third part of his report, Doveri proposes changes "to return the Temple as much as possible to its primitive state."[22] These changes include replacing the nineteenth-century windows circling the cupola with windows in a thirteenth-century style; removing the Baroque altars that line the walls of the side aisles and opening up the medieval windows that they block; and taking out the Baroque sculptures mounted on the columns of the nave and supporting the cupola. When he took over as Cathedral architect in 1866,

Partini dedicated himself to carrying out many of Doveri's plans. Influenced by the religiosity of the *puristi* and the work of Viollet-le-Duc, Partini removed Baroque altars and sculptures, reshaped windows, and put stained glass in dozens of others in order to bring the Siena Cathedral back to its medieval state. Partini describes his particular approach to restoration in a proposal he prepared in 1883 for Rubini, the rector of the cathedral, concerning the enlargement of the cathedral's clerestory windows.[23] In keeping with Doveri's ideas, Partini argues that Mazzuoli's statues of the twelve Apostles and the Virgin and Christ must be removed because they interrupt the expansiveness of the nave and therefore interfere with the original intentions of the architects, and that the altars blocking the windows in the side aisles of the nave must be removed so that the medieval windows could be reopened and adorned with historiated stained glass windows to bathe the side aisles in dark light.[24]

For Partini, an even larger goal than removing the Baroque additions to the cathedral was the lightening of the interior. The central goal of Partini's 1883 report was to convince Rubini that the clerestory windows in the nave from the cupola to the altar must also be enlarged. To persuade him, Partini writes that, with the newly enlarged clerestory in the front of the church, "...thanks to the light that shines down, one can now admire the famous painting of Pinturicchio of the Coronation of Pius II...: this painting, because it was in such darkness before the reopening of the windows, could have been considered as lost to the eyes of visitors."[25] Partini here appeals to Rubini's Sienese pride: he notes the famous fresco of the Sienese pope, and praises the wealth of art contained in the cathedral. The enlargement of the windows in the east end, therefore, would illuminate the Pisano pulpit, much as the Pinturicchio fresco was revealed by the earlier project. In addition to making the great monuments of Sienese art more visible, Partini maintains that the enlargement of the clerestory windows would provide a more spiritual environment. Near the beginning of the report, Partini refers to Viollet-le-Duc's restoration of medieval churches in France, which Partini believed were carried out with "faithful scrupulousness" and with "exquisite taste." In Partini's view, Viollet-le-Duc's goal was to concentrate light in upper parts of the church, in the clerestory, and leave the nave in semi-obscurity, lit only by the darkly colored light of stained glass windows.[26] As it did in the Middle Ages, Partini hoped that the celestial light of the clerestory windows, coupled with the relative darkness of the nave, would create a profound sense of feeling and religious devotion in the hearts of nineteenth-century Catholics. The worshipper's gaze should be drawn upwards, toward heaven and the light of the clerestory windows. The recreation of what Partini believed to be the original medieval state of the building was therefore an almost sacred obligation.

Partini's report evidently convinced Rubini: from 1883-85, a team of masons and sculptors worked to enlarge all of the clerestory windows in the east end and outfit each one with an elaborate marble armature in a Gothic style.[27] The same work had already been carried out on the clerestory windows in the western nave of the church from 1881-83. The enlargement of the cathedral's entire clerestory was no small task. The lower parts of the windows were obscured when the roof of the side aisles was raised in the later fourteenth century; in order to enlarge the windows, the nineteenth-century restorers had to cut through the roof of the side aisle and form an exterior window well.[28] De Matteis made all of the stained glass for the newly enlarged clerestory windows, each consisting of clear bull's eye glass adorned with small blue and red seraphim. The clear glass allows for a great deal of light to shine through, in keeping with Partini's spiritual aims for the enlargement of the clerestory. The bull's eye windows were also relatively cheap to produce, because De Matteis did not have to create elaborate designs that would take excessive time to formulate and execute.[29] The Siena clerestory windows in the east end of the nave are more complex in design. They consist of clear bull's eye glass, again allowing bright light to shine through, with the coats-of-arms and portraits of Sienese popes in the center part of each window. The window dedicated to Leo XIII, for example, shows a portrait bust medallion of the pope in the center, with papal and familial coats of arms surrounding him. The inclusion of Sienese popes in the window iconography was Rubini's idea: in the summer of 1885, he wrote to the Pope asking for money for these new windows, which would depict "the images of the venerable pontiffs who were from Siena and its ancient State."[30] The papal theme of De Matteis' windows links them to the fifteenth-century sculpted images of pontiffs that line the cathedral walls just below the clerestory.

While Partini was able to realize his luminous goals for the clerestory of the cathedral, the darkly lit gloom he hoped to create in the earthly regions of the cathedral was never achieved. Although Partini's successor as cathedral architect, Agenore Socini, intended to remove the Baroque altars, they remain to this day in the cathedral's side aisles. Partini nonetheless was able to place two historiated stained glass windows in the lower part of the church: in the 1880s, under Rubini's direction, a fifteenth-century stained glass window composed of six standing figures was taken from the suppressed convent of San Francesco in Colle Val d'Elsa, divided in two halves, each composed of three standing figures, and placed in the left and right transepts of Siena Cathedral.[31] The window was first sent from Colle Val d'Elsa to Florence, where De Matteis examined it, cleaned the glass and replaced all of the window's leading. The window was then sent back to Siena and installed in the cathedral in 1885. Only the section of the Colle Val d'Elsa window placed in the left transept survives today, and its iconography betrays its Franciscan origins: the top figure is St. Francis, with St. Blaise and St. Anthony of Padua below.[32] The documents do not indicate why Rubini and Partini brought the fifteenth-century Colle Val d'Elsa window to Siena, and it is somewhat unexpected that the architects would decide to place an early Renaissance window in a thirteenth-century architectural environment that they were consciously restoring to a medieval state.[33] However, the remaining window does have the desired effect described by Partini in the 1883 report: despite the predominance of white glass, the various shades of blue, red, gold and brown dark in the window glass surround the viewer with a dark luminosity. Perhaps with the reopening of a medieval window and the installation of a historiated stained glass window, Partini was able to accomplish on a small scale what he had hoped to establish in all the side aisles of the nave.

In the early 1890s, Partini commissioned De Matteis to create twelve stained glass panels depicting the Apostles for the windows in the drum of the cupola.[34] The color palette of these windows, composed predominantly of deep blues, reds and green, and the composition of the windows, made of figures standing under elaborate Gothic tabernacles, resemble Tuscan and Umbrian stained glass of the fourteenth-century, such as the windows in the basilica of San Francesco in Assisi, San Domenico in Perugia, and the Duomo and Santa Croce in Florence. Because he knew the windows intimately, De Matteis turned in particular to the stained glass of Santa Croce. In the Siena windows, De Matteis mimicked the tri-lobed arcades of the Bardi St. Francis window from ca. 1325, located above the Bardi chapel just to the right of the high altar in Santa Croce.[35] The prevalent blues, reds and golds in the Siena windows mirror those of the Bardi window, and the green details in the Siena window are closer to the palette of the stained glass in the high altar chapel of Santa Croce, created ca. 1388-93.[36] While De Matteis loosely based the tabernacles that surmount the Siena apostles on those in the Santa Croce high altar windows, he directly copied Santa Croce's geometric borders of gold, green, red and white geometric shapes for the borders surrounding several of the Siena apostles. He might have looked to thirteenth-century examples of stained glass in Italy—the large rose (designed possibly by Duccio) in the Siena cathedral itself and the apse glazing of the upper church of San Francesco in Assisi are closer in date to the cathedral's architecture.[37] However, the medallion and narrative format of these early windows were not well suited to the slender lancets of the Siena cathedral drum because any intricate figural or decorative work would not be visible from the ground. Not only was the composition of standing figures under Gothic tabernacles chosen by De Matteis for the Siena Apostle windows legible at significant heights, it was also the most common type of medieval window in Italy beginning in the early fourteenth century.[38] Moreover, in De Matteis and

Partini's day, this type of window became synonymous with Italian medieval stained glass. The composition and color palette of the Apostle windows, based closely on fourteenth-century examples from Santa Croce, were appropriate choices for the recreation of the medieval cathedral.

To create the spiritual atmosphere outlined in his 1883 report, Partini wanted to commission darkly colored stained glass windows for the windows of the Siena cathedral's side aisles. Although he was not able to do so, most likely prohibited by the enormous scale of his proposed renovations and the attendant bureaucracy, other churches in Siena proved more hospitable to Partini's vision of the medieval church. In Santa Maria dei Servi and San Francesco, for example, Partini was able to accomplish on a smaller scale what he envisioned for the cathedral. In the case of San Francesco, the funding of many private patrons made the restoration possible, and at Santa Maria dei Servi, the local parish was the driving force behind Partini's work.

In 1882, the city commission on Fine Arts named Partini as the director of the San Francesco church restoration. Following a fire in 1655, the Gothic windows in the church had been either completely closed up, with Baroque altars placed in front of them, or filled in enough to leave only a rectangular opening.[39] The medieval church had suffered further indignity when it became a military barracks during the wars for independence in the late 1850s and 1860s. By the 1870s, the Sienese began to call for the return of the church to its antique form. Partini did just that: he took all of the Baroque altars and other decorative elements out of the church, opened up all of the closed windows, and re-made them into pointed, Gothic windows filled with historiated stained glass. A total of 35 windows were needed to completely glaze the church, and the commission was split between De Matteis and the Zettler firm of Munich.[40] Zettler's window of the *Approval of the Rule* survives, but much of the other nineteenth-century windows, including all of De Matteis', were lost in World War II. A large proportion of the expense incurred by the 19th-century restoration was due to this large number of windows, indicating the importance of stained glass to Partini's idea of the medieval church interior.[41] When Partini's plan was completed in 1894, the effect must have been fabulous: the large, barn-like nave, filled with new stained glass, glowed with the dark light that Partini had desired for the cathedral's side aisles.

Like San Francesco, the church of Santa Maria dei Servi was built in the mid thirteenth century and extensively restored in the sixteenth and seventeenth centuries, when much of the fourteenth- and fifteenth-century decoration was either painted over or taken out and the pointed, Gothic windows were walled up and altars were placed in front of them.[42] In 1886, the parish of the Servi commissioned Partini to restore one of apse chapels "to its antique splendor," as a contemporary newspaper reported.[43] The success of this project prompted the restoration of much of the transept, in particular the high altar chapel.[44] In 1894, De Matteis' five stained glass windows were installed in the restored Gothic aperatures in the apse of the church. The windows were based on drawings made by the painter Alessandro Franchi, a student and close friend of the purist Luigi Mussini. The program of windows consists of a heavenly chorus of the saints most important to the Servite order, with the Virgin's Assumption in the top center lancet. The standing saints, forming the majority of the program, resemble other contemporary works by De Matteis, including the Apostles at the base of the cupola in the Siena cathedral and the apse window in the church of Santa Trinita in Florence, which in turn reflected fourteenth-century Florentine models carried out in the Gothic tabernacle style. Although the figural aspects of the Servi windows were based on the drawings of a painter, De Matteis worked like a medieval glazier and consciously incorporated the color scheme and overall design of fourteenth-century stained glass into his work.[45] The Servi windows are exceptionally well crafted, and their high quality and medieval style met Partini's goals for the restoration project quite well. Not only did they emulate the work of the medieval craftsman, a central goal of Partini's restoration, but the hovering chorus of saints also creates a dark, warm light that provides a mystical feeling in the apse area and transept. The spiritually charged, colored light is close to what Partini hoped to create on a much larger scale in the nave of the Siena cathedral.

The long-standing collaboration and friendship between Partini and De Matteis indicate the importance of light, and of colored light in particular, to Partini's architectural purism. Partini did not attempt to recreate the original cathedral interior based solely on archaeological evidence; instead, through his restorations, he strove to inspire spiritual devotion in those who visited the cathedral. As he wrote to Rubini in 1883, Partini wanted to emulate the medieval architect, who, motivated by love instead of architectural theory, sought to create spiritual church environments. The darkly lit gloom of the cathedral side aisles, coupled with the light streaming in from the enlarged clerestory, was intended to bring nineteenth-century worshippers back to a medieval religious state, to a "pure" spiritualism that Partini believed had been lost in Tuscany in the post-medieval period. However, the evocation of a medieval religiosity was not Partini's only purpose: by restoring and recreating the medieval monuments of Siena, Partini also celebrated the time of medieval *comune*, the period before the Medici dukes ruled Tuscany. Partini literally attempted to excise the Baroque period, closely associated by the purists with the Medici and Habsburg dukes of Tuscany, from Siena Cathedral, San Francesco and Santa Mari dei Servi by removing the Baroque additions to their interiors and return them to a "pure" medieval state. The work of De Matteis played an instrumental role in Partini's efforts; with the Baroque altars and sculptures removed from these medieval churches, De Matteis' windows, which were consistently praised for their fidelity to the techniques and aesthetics of medieval stained glass, played a prominent role in creating the religious atmosphere Partini desired. By restoring and recreating the monuments of the Middle Ages, Partini and De Matteis elevated medieval Siena to a place of religious, artistic and political superiority.

ST. OLAF COLLEGE

NOTES

[1] This article was first presented as a paper at the International Congress on Medieval Studies at Kalamazoo, Michigan on May 8, 2004.

[2] The two likely met in the mid 1860s, when De Matteis made windows for the chapel of S. Giovanni in the Siena cathedral, and they collaborated quite frequently until Partini's death. On the restoration of the chapel of S. Giovanni, see Ferdinando Rubini, *Dei restauri eseguiti nella chiesa Metropolitana di Siena dal luglio 1864 all'agosto 1869* (Siena, 1869). For a summary of Rubini's account, see Giuseppe Cruciani Fabozzi, "La storia tradita: guida ai monumenti infedeli d'Italia: il duomo di Siena," *L'architettura* 322/323 (1981): 616. Documents pertaining to the restoration can be found in the Archivio dell'Opera di Santa Maria di Siena (AOMS), Lavori e restauri straordinari straordinari, Registro generale dei lavori eseguiti, Filza 1629 [2], Cappella di S. Giovanni. Natale Bruschi and Ulisse De Matteis, who both worked for the Francini company in Florence, are listed as *"fabricanti di vetri a smalto colorati."*

[3] Cristina Buscioni, *Giuseppe Partini: Architetto del Purismo senese* (Florence, 1981), pp. 59-63, gives a brief biography of Partini. See also Vittorio Mariani, *L'architetto Giuseppe Partini* (Siena, 1921) and idem, *In memoria di Giuseppe Partini* (Siena, 1924).

[4] Buscioni, p. 59 and G.A. Reycend, *Cenni commemorativi dell'Architetto Giuseppe Partini* (Turin, 1896), p. 3.

[5] On Partini's early commissions, see Buscioni, pp. 141-45.

[6] Buscioni, p. 59.

[7] Luigi Mussini, "Sullo studio de' maestri antichi e sugli ostacoli che ad esso si frappongono," in *Scritti d'arte di Luigi Mussini, pittore* (Florence, 1880), pp. 3-13. Originally written in 1847.

[8] See Luigi Mussini, *In memoria di Luigi Mussini pittore* (Siena, 1888), pp. 1-16, for a brief biography of Mussini and a list of his major artistic and literary works. In *Epistolario artistico di Luigi Mussini* (Siena 1893), Mussini's daughter Luisa Anzoletti gives a more personal biography of her father, followed by many of his letters. For a discussion of Mussini's career, see Giovanna Uzzani, "Luigi Mussini: formazione purista ed esiti senesi," in *Siena tra purismo e liberty*, ed. Bernardina Sani (Milan, 1988), pp. 81-86. Cesare Guasti, in his essay "Del purismo nell'arte a proposito di un quadro di Luigi Mussini," first published in Florence in 1851 and reprinted in his *Scritti d'arte* (Prato, 1897), pp. 53-61, outlines the concepts embraced by the *puristi*.

[9] Norma Broude, *The Macchaioli: Italian Painters of the Nineteenth Century* (New Haven and London, 1987), p. 24.

[10] Broude, 24.

[11] The Macchiaioli painters in Florence are often connected with the politics of the Risorgimento. See Broude and Albert Boime, *The Art of the Macchia and the Risorgimento* (Chicago and London, 1993). For background on the historical circumstances of the Risorgimento, see Boime, pp. 19-39; Harry Hearder, *Italy in the Age of the Risorgimento 1790-1870* (London, 1983); and Lucy Riall, *The Italian Risorgimento: State, society and national unification* (New York, 1994).

[12] The 1915 catalog also gives a brief history of the firm. *Officina De Matteis vetraria: per la costruzione e per il restauro di vetrate dipinte a smalto a gran fuoco, secondo il sistema degli antichi maestri*, hereafter referred to as *Officina De Matteis*. A copy of this catalog exists in the Archivio Storico Comunale di Firenze (ASCF), Filza 5064, Palazzo della Posta. When Ulisse De Matteis died in 1910, the firm was taken over by his son-in-law, the painter Ezio Giovanozzi, who married Rita De Matteis in 1909. De Matteis had hoped that his son Sergio and daughter Eva would lead the family business, but Sergio died in 1907 and Eva in 1908.

[13] Antonio Pavan, "Della pittura su vetro e del laboratorio De Matteis in Firenze,"*Arte in Italia* II (1870): 68-9.

[14] Pavan, p. 68. For the list of prizes, see "Classe XI: arte vetraria e ceramica," *L'esposizione italiana del 1861*, (Florence, 1862), pp. 278-79. Documents concerning the 1859-61 restoration of the façade window are in the Archivio della Curia in San Miniato (ACV), coll.1546, vol. 1, "Restauri del Duomo." Some of these documents are published by Roberta Villani in "Restauri a San Miniato al Tedesco: documenti per una storia," *Bollettino dell'Accadema degli Euleti di San Miniato al Tedesco* 63 (1996): 163-93. See also Dilvio Lotti, *San Miniato: vita di un'antica città* (Genoa, 1980).

[15] According to the documents in the Archivio della Curia, San Miniato, the opera wanted De Matteis (who then worked for the Francini company) to work with the extant fragments. The fragments were likely too corroded and would have clashed with the clear, new glass.

[16] For the Ghiberti window, see Giuseppe Marchini, *Italian Stained Glass Windows* (Milan, 1956), plate 42. See also the Italian Stained Glass Windows Database: http://www.area.fi.cnr.it/bivi/schede/Toscana/Firenze/6cattedrale1.htm. Link verified July 28, 2005.

[17] On the history of the chapel decoration, see Walter and Elisabeth Paatz, *Die Kirchen von Florenz* 1 (Frankfurt-am-Main, 1940), pp. 572-73.

[18] Luigi Mussini, "Les travaux de restauration de l'église de Santa Croce a Florence," in *Scritti d'arte di Luigi Mussini, pittore* (Florence, 1880), pp. 208-9. This paper was originally read at the French Institute on February 2, 1870 and published in *L'art* XVIII (1879): 258-60. Mussini notes that Mr. Sloane endowed his chapel, the Spinelli-Sloane chapel just to the left of the apse, with a beautiful stained glass window. For more on the Bardi Holy Confessors window, see Nancy Thompson, "The Fourteenth-Century Stained Glass of Santa Croce in Florence," (Indiana University, 1999), pp. 47-49, on the stylistic origins of the window, pp. 142-48 on the iconography of the window and its place in the decorative program of the chapel, and pp. 207-12 on the current condition of the window. For color images of the Bardi window, see Giuseppe Marchini, "Le vetrate," in *Complesso monumentale di Sta. Croce: la basilica, le capelle, i chiostri*, eds., U. Baldini and B. Nardini (Florence, 1983), pp. 320-21See also the Italian Stained Glass

Windows Database: http://server.icvbc.cnr.it/bivi/schede/Toscana/Firenze/15scroce. htm. Link verified July 28, 2005.

[19] The entire inscription on the left wall of the chapel asserts, "Questa cappella già dei Tolosini poi degli Spinelli e degli Sloane che nel 1560 e dopo parì i danni della decadenza dell'arte fù nel 1869 ritornata alla antica forma seguendo le tracce della prima costruzione del 1295. Si conservarono per la storia della pittura gli affreschi del Martellini dipinti nel 1837." Sloane and the restorers evidently did not approve of Vasari's sixteenth-century interventions in the church.

[20] Mussini, "Les travaux de restauration," p. 214. The restoration of Santa Trinita in Florence, initiated in 1881 by Giuseppe Poggi and Emilio de Fabris, was approached in a similar way, although the Santa Trinita restorers were much more systematic. They completely stripped the church of its Baroque decoration, despite the protests many Florentines and the English press. See Marco Bardeschi and Maria Masetti, "La storia tradita: guida ai monumenti infedeli d'Italia. La chiesa di S. Trinita a Firenze," L'architettura: cronache e storia XXVII/12 (1981): 720-25. Bardeschi and Masetti also sum up the stages of the restoration and the controversy it raised. For a blow-by-blow account of the various restorations of the church, see chapters six through eight of La chiesa di Santa Trinita a Firenze, eds. Giuseppe Marchini and Emma Micheletti (Florence, 1987), pp. 61-88, especially chapter six by Monica Maffioli, "La querelle ottocenttesca per il restauro della chiesa: dalle teorie al contiere," pp. 61-70.

[21] AOMS, Lavori e restauri straordinari, Carteggio e atti 1824-1890, Filza 1626,1866-1890 [69], "Relazione, e respettiva Perizia Sullo Stato ed ammontare dei più urgenti bisogni occorenti della Fabbrica del Duomo di Siena; sia per la parte Statica e Decorativa; sia per la parte della Decenza, e Conservazione di un Monumento Artistico, consacrato al Culto Divino compilata Dall'Architetto Professor Lorenzo Doveri il di 15 Febbrajo 1860." For a summary of Doveri's proposal, see Cruciano Fabozzi, p. 616.

[22] Doveri titled the third section of his report, "Variazioni che propongo di fare per restituire quel Tempio il più possibile al suo primitivo stato."

[23] Giuseppe Partini, "Lavori di restauro che resterebbero ad eseguirsi nella nostra cattedrale, onde ritornarla al suo antico splendore 1883/1886," AOMS Carteggio, atti e copialettere, Affari diversi 1770-1915, Filza 159 [2]. I would like to thank Dr. Wolfgang Losieres of the Kunsthistorisches Institut in Florence for sharing documents and photographs from his work on the unpublished volume three of Die Kirchen von Siena, which will focus on the Cathedral.

[24] Rubini was evidently puzzled by Partini's desire to remove Mazzuoli's sculptures. Mussini, in true purist fashion, viewed them as "Baroque invaders," and lobbied for their removal. The sculptures were not removed until after Rubin's death in 1890; however, their iconography was preserved with De Matteis' windows of the twelve Apostles (discussed below) made for the lower part of the dome in the late 1880s. See Cruciani Fabozzi, pp. 619-20.

[25] AOMS Carteggio, atti e copialettere, Affari diversi 1770-1915, Filza 159 [2]. "Intanto argomentando dagli effetti ottenuti con la riapertura già eseguita delle dieci finestre superiori della navata centrale, mercè la luce che esse tramandano, può ora ammirarsi nuovamente il famoso dipinto del Pinturicchio raffigurante l'incoronazione di Pio II, e che esiste al disopra della porta di accesso alla Libreria Piccolominea: quale dipinto, per l'oscurità in cui rimaneva avvolto prima della riapertua di quei finestroni poteva considerarsi come perduta agli sguardi dei visitatori."

[26]AOMS Carteggio, atti e copialettere, Affari diversi 1770-1915, Filza 159 [2]. "Ed invero, nei monumenti congeneri di origine mediovale, non solo in Italia ma anche in Francia ove dal celebre Viollet-le-Duc sono stati eseguiti restauri di chiese con fedeltà scrupolosa, e con un gusto veramente squisito, si riscontra costante applicazione del sistema di raccogliere molta luce nella parte superiore, con una semi oscurità in basso, ottenuta col mezzo di finestre riccamente storiate con vetri a foschi colori. È tutto ciò, non già per intuito di mera parvenza, ma sibbene per il duplice quanto mirabile effetto, di fare apparire maggiore l'elevatezza del tempio, e di infondere nell'ambiente quel non so che di mistico e di solenne che in tempi di schietto e forte sentire aveva un eco profondo negli animi compresi di fede religiosa fervida quanto sincera, ma non manca di efficacia neppure ai di nostri, perché in ogni mente colta ed in ogni cuore gentile ha, ed avrà sempre un'azione arcana ed irresistibile quella sapiente combinazione di luce che mentre invita all'ascetico raccoglimento con la queta penombra che regna a terreno, attira lo sguardo, e con lo sguardo la mente alla vivida luce che piove dall'alto."

[27] Documents concerning the opening of the masonry and the making of the stained glass windows are preserved in the cathedral archive. "Finestroni riaperti sul Cornicione Della navate centrale eseguito della Ditta Mattei di Firenze (1885)," AOMS, Carteggio, atti e copialettere, Affari diversi 1770-1915, 159, 1875-1919 [15]. A series of letters in the folder from De Matteis to Rubini records the struggle between Rubini and De Matteis concerning payment for and the timely completion of the clerestory windows.

[28] See Tim Benton, "The Design of Siena and Florence Duomos," in *Siena, Florence and Padua: Art, Society and Religion 1280-1400*, Vol. 2, ed. Diana Norman (New Haven and London, 1995), pp. 129-43.

[29] De Matteis most commonly produced this type of window for large-scale commissions; for example, De Matteis and the Francini company produced dozens of bull's eye glass windows for the Bargello in Florence in the early 1860s. On the Bargello restoration, see Giovanna Gaeta Bertelà, "Il restauro del Palazzo del Podestà," in *Studi e ricerche di collezionismo e museografia Firenze 1820-1920* (Pisa, 1985), pp. 179-209 and Beatrice Paolizzi Strozzi, ed., *La storia del Bargello: 100 capolavori di scoprire* (Florence, 2004).

[30] Cruciani Fabozzi, p. 619, n. 35.

[31] For documentation on the window's removal, restoration, and reinstallation in the Siena Cathedral, see AOMS Carteggio, atti e copialettere, Affari diversi, 158 [40], "Vetrata Istoriata Proveniente dal soppresso Convento di S. Francesco in Colle" and "Rimozione di altari e apertura di una finestrone nel fianco destro della Cattedrale (1877-1883)."

[32] Elio Manna, *Guida storico-artistica del Duomo di Siena* (Siena, 1908), pp. 124-25 and Virgilio Grassi, *Guida storico-artistico del Duomo di Siena e sue adiacenze* (Siena, 1924), pp. 20 and 26. Both describe the window that was once in the right transept; it contained images of St. Bonaventure, St. Bernard and St. Louis.

[33] The convent was no longer active when the window was removed. Perhaps the window was slated to be removed from San Francesco during a restoration and the Sienese chose to preserve it in their cathedral. It is also possible that the window was the closest and oldest one Partini and Rubini could find that would suit their needs in restoring their Cathedral.

[34] These windows preserved the iconography of the Mazzuoli sculptures that had recently been removed. See Cruciani Fabozzi, p. 620. For documents concerning the commission, see "Vetrate

della Cupola (1866-1888)," AOMS Carteggio, atti e copialettere, Affari diversi 1770-1915, 159 [10] (Casella 16). There is a brief correspondence in the 1860s between the Francini glass company (for whom De Matteis worked) and Rubini concerning stained glass windows for the drum of the cupola. Apparently this commission was not completed, and correspondence about the extant windows began in 1886. De Matteis also made the eight windows in the lantern of the cupola. For documents concerning the commission, see "Vetrate per la laterna della cupola ordinate al prof. Ulisse De Matteis, e per il lavoro del fabbro (1888-1893),"Carteggio, Atti e Copialettere, Carteggio e atti diversi in fascicoli annuali 1871-1920, 101 [4] (ins. 14).

[35] For a color image of the Bardi St. Francis window, see Marchini 1983, p.317. See also the Italian Stained Glass Windows Database: http://server.icvbc.cnr.it/bivi/schede/Toscana/Firenze/7scroce.htm. Link verified July 28, 2005.

[36] For more on the fourteenth-century stained glass and image program of Santa Croce's high altar chapel, see Nancy Thompson, "St. Francis, the Apocalypse and the True Cross: The Decoration of the *Cappella Maggiore* of Santa Croce in Florence," *Gesta* XLIII/1 (2004): 61-79.

[37] On the Siena rose window, see Enzo Carli, *Vetrata duccesca* (Florence, 1956) and John White, *Art and Architecture in Italy 1250-1400*, 3rd ed. (New Haven and London, 1993). For an account of the recent restoration of the rose, see Alessando Bagnoli and Camillo Tarozzi, *Duccio: La vetrate del Duomo di Siena e il suo restauro* (Milan, 2003). See also the Italian Stained Glass Windows Database: http://server.icvbc.cnr.it/bivi/schede/Toscana/siena/1cattedrale.htm. Link verified July 28, 2005. On the Assisi glass, see Giuseppe Marchini, *Le vetrate dell'Umbria*, Corpus Vitrearum Medii Aevi, Italia I (Rome, 1973) and Frank Martin and P. Gerhard Ruf, *Die Glasmalereien von San Francesco in Assisi: Entstehung und Entwicklung einer Gattung in Italien* (Regensburg, 1997). See also the Italian Stained Glass Windows Database: http://server.icvbc.cnr.it/bivi/schede/Umbria/Assisi/1sanfrancesco_sup.htm. Link verified July 28, 2005.

[38] The author, in chapter two of her dissertation "The Fourteenth-Century Stained Glass of Santa Croce in Florence," discusses the development of the tabernacle window in Italy.

[39] Buscioni, 179-81 and Vittorio Lusini, *Storia della basilica di S. Francesco in Siena* (Siena, 1894), p. 274.

[40] Lusini, p. 260. Lusini includes a list of all of the artists and patrons of the stained glass created for San Francesco's restoration.

[41] Lusini outlines the entire cost of the restoration.

[42] In his brief report, "I restauri alla chiesa dei Servi di Maria in Siena," *Arte e storia* 23-24 XVIII (1899): 150-52, Guido Carocci reports that Baldassare Peruzzi restored the church from 1511-28.

[43] Buscioni, p. 183.

[44] The restoration continued after Partini's death in 1895 under his student Agnore Socini and was not complete until the first years of the twentieth century.

[45] This method, where the glazier carries out the design of a painter, was typical of the medieval and Renaissance periods in Italy. The painter was usually responsible only for the figural aspects of the window; the glazier had to translate the drawing into a viable stained glass window and incorporate decorative details and a color scheme appropriate for the medium. See Renée Karen Burnam, "Medieval Stained Glass Practice in Florence, Italy: the Case of Orsanmichele," *Journal of Glass Studies* XXX (1988): 77-93.

From Life to Legend:
Nationalism and the Image of Edward the Black Prince

Barbara Gribling

The same year had seen the death of [Edward III's] eldest son Edward, Prince of Wales and Aquitaine, the flower of the world's knighthood and at that time the most successful soldier of his age. This most gallant man and chivalrous prince died at the palace of Westminster…on the eighth of June 1376.
The Chronicles of Froissart, c. 1376-1378

> The Black Prince, noble and doughty warrior, mounted on his
> magnificent charger, life-like and full of action, stood out
> prominently…he looked the hero of a hundred fights, the noble
> conqueror who first placed England among the premier nations
> of the world, the flower of English chivalry, the upholder
> of the people's rights, the idol of the nation.
> *The Leeds and Yorkshire Mercury, September 17ᵗʰ, 1903*

On the 8th of June, 1376, Edward, Prince of Wales and Aquitaine, died in London. In his chronicles, Jean Froissart of Hainault presented Edward as a world-class knight who embodied the chivalric values and ideals of an entire aristocratic community. When describing Edward's death, Froissart confirmed the established medieval image of the prince as a transnational hero of the nobility. In the Victorian and Edwardian period, however, this medieval image was transformed when elites, historians, artists, and authors began constructing the prince as a national hero and framing him within the mold of an English gentleman. The completed transition to gentleman national hero is apparent in the 1903 statue of Edward, the Black Prince that was unveiled in Leeds City Square. The equestrian bronze was a gift from Colonel T. Walter Harding to the people of Leeds in celebration of the fact that Leeds had gained city status. This statue represented the culmination of the Victorian and early Edwardian vision of the medieval prince as an English gentleman in all of his various roles: as a moralist, a politician, and a military man. According to the *Leeds and Yorkshire Mercury*, as noted above, Edward was a moral hero whose persona was emblematic of a multitude of English virtues. He was also a politician who championed the rights of the English people, particularly during the Good Parliament of 1376.[1] He was an important military figure whose victories in battle at Crécy in 1346 and at Poitiers in 1356 encouraged patriotism and contributed to England's growth as a European power. This essay examines how Victorian and Edwardian elites, historians, and authors reinvented the image of the fourteenth-century prince by presenting him as a gentleman—a key icon of English national identity. In particular, the paper focuses on one aspect of Edward's gentlemanly image: his role as a military hero.

How can the prince's different images be understood within and across their historical and cultural contexts? Theorist Benedict Anderson's concept of an imagined community offers one possible explanation. Anderson suggests that, in the Middle Ages, communities were linked together through their common religion and by large dynasties that stretched over broad territories.[2] Within this larger Christian community, the prince was promoted as a member of a more specific group of knights. The prince was thus fashioned as a transnational hero, a hero whose image was promoted beyond the confines of national borders—in this instance, across the medieval European world. Yet the promotion of his image was intended for a particular aristocratic audience. In the medieval chronicles, the prince had more in common with other European aristocrats—shared language, values, and blood ties—than he did with the English peasant classes, for example. Therefore, while the prince belonged to the larger medieval Christian community, his image belonged to a more specific yet still transnational aristocratic class.

In nineteenth-century England, the prince's apotheosis as a national hero can be linked to the wider European process of modernization and to the experience of modernity itself. When the larger religious European communities collapsed, new national communities were imagined. Scholars Marshall Berman, Matei Calinescu and Harry Harootunian state that, as nations underwent the process of modernization through urbanization, capitalism, and industrialization, members of nations felt increasingly isolated from each other. This disconnection, known as the experience of modernity, created the feeling that time was moving forward at an increasing pace; for many, the present felt devoid of meaning.[3] To compensate for this experience of modern discontinuity, nationalists searched for new ways to create a horizontal national identity. Officials constructed national heroes to link the English community together. English nationalists who promoted past and present heroes focussed on the Black Prince—in part, because his image could be easily adapted to the values of the time.

The growing preoccupation with the Middle Ages and its heroes can also be placed within a larger European debate about the origins and nature of the nation itself. It was during this time that the nation as a concept with roots in antiquity developed. Members of nations could feel bonded together through their common past and a common future. The English interest in the Middle Ages was related to nationalists' desire to create this common past through reworking medieval heroes. This also explains how the prince's image can be both past, as in part of England's heroic past, and present, in that his admirable qualities were seen to live on in contemporary Victorians.

The origins of Edward's transformation into a national hero can be seen as early as the sixteenth century. For example, William Shakespeare's *Henry V* presents the prince as part of the English national community by contrasting the heroic Edward with his antiheroic French enemies. In the late seventeenth and eighteenth centuries, the prince's national image continued to evolve and historians frequently described Edward as the people's prince. Eighteenth-century historian Arthur Collins confirmed this new vision of Edward, writing that the prince "has ever been the Darling of our Nation" to which "all Ranks of people" have applauded.[4] This increased emphasis on the prince's good relations with the English people is most easily seen in the lauding of the prince's relationship to parliament. However, it was not until the Victorian period that the prince's image as a national hero was fully developed, for it was only then that the prince was fashioned into a gentleman.

It was during the Victorian era that nationalists developed the image of the English gentleman as a key icon of English identity. This development can be directly related to contemporary debates in cultural circles about the apparent decline of the English character. Nationalists promoted the gentlemanly lifestyle as a way to counter the negative conditions of industrialization and modernity. The "gentleman" image can be simultaneously linked to the growth of empire, wherein gentlemen venture out into the world to "civilize" members of other nations. Edward's representation as a gentleman hero, a form only fully developed in the nineteenth century, led to his position as the quintessential national hero.

In contrast to this Victorian national identity, fourteenth-century chroniclers such as Jean Froissart established a vision of the prince as a transnational class hero; the key aim of Froissart's *Chronicles* was, in fact, to illustrate the chivalrous acts of all European knights.[5] In his description of the battle of Crécy, Froissart praised the actions of the sixteen-year-old prince, who, finding himself in the midst of battle, bravely fought French troops. Froissart also praised the bravery of John, the blind king of Bohemia, who sided with the French at Crécy. According to Froissart, John's loyal knights tied their horses to his, leading him into battle and allowing the king to perform chivalrous acts. Froissart mourned the fact that so many brave and noble knights died on both sides at Crécy, including the blind king of Bohemia. In his medieval chronicles, all European knights had the opportunity to perform the virtues of prowess, nobility, generosity, and wisdom on an international stage.[6] Nowhere were these qualities more appreciated than on the battlefield. In the fourteenth century, then, the prince was considered to be a heroic European knight, and his performance was celebrated throughout the medieval world.

In contrast, in the nineteenth century, English nationalists interested in the Black Prince reinvented his military role by presenting him as an English gentleman. In his 1903 play, Maurice Baring emphasized the prince's martial prowess by comparing Edward to the fearless St. George, patron saint of England and a legendary warrior whose military feats included the slaying of a dragon.[7] Baring suggested that Edward's heroic feats at the battles of Crécy and Poitiers were as worthy of fame as England's own patron saint. More importantly, Baring nationalized Edward's battle skills by reframing the prince's prowess and gentlemanly modesty as specifically English characteristics.

While in the fourteenth century French and English knights were equally celebrated for their noble deeds, by the nineteenth nationalism had changed the English perception of the French.[8] English citizens were looking for an "other," a country with which to compare themselves with in order to cement their national identity.[9] The English emphasized the differences between themselves and the French and tried to show that their English religion, language, race, and culture were superior to this constructed Gallic "other."

Given this cultural and political context, Victorian authors and historians often vilified and mocked the French nobles. In Victorian histories, plays, and stories about the Black Prince, the French were depicted in an unflattering light. In her *Story of Edward the Black Prince,* Meredith Jones presented the French at the battle of Poitiers as vain and cowardly, as compared to the courageous English forces under Prince Edward.[10] Jones showed the famous French knight Geoffrey of Charny as a "scheming Frenchman," and she chastised King Charles of France for not keeping his word.[11] In the Black Prince literature of the nineteenth century, the gentleman prince usually appeared virtuous and brave, in comparison to his effeminate, cowardly, and deceitful French enemies.[12]

Unlike this Victorian casting of the French as the "other," in the late Middle Ages, the war with France was considered to be a struggle between rival relatives vying for the French throne, rather than a national conflict. In their chronicles and poems, fourteenth-century authors emphasized similarities between European knights. English knights in the fourteenth century spoke the same language as their French counterparts, and many English knights held lands in France. When describing the beginning of the war, Froissart focuses on presenting King Edward III as a monarch concerned with regaining his rightful inheritance from his relative the King of France: the French crown.[13]

In the nineteenth century, the Hundred Years' War was reframed from a nationalist perspective. In fact, the term itself was invented in the 1860s to describe the dynastic wars that lasted from 1337-1453.[14] Nineteenth-century scholars thus redefined the war as a nationalist struggle between England and France, and these scholars used the Hundred Years' War to emphasize the differences between the English and their "other." Entire chapters in nineteenth

century histories are devoted to the Hundred Years War and its significance as a
prolonged national event rather than as a series of dynastic battles.[15] Thus, this
new concept of the Hundred Years War became an integral part of England's
national story, alongside the fourteenth-century growth of parliament and the
development of the English language.

As the fear of French invasion dissipated, in the late nineteenth century,
the English continued to celebrate Edward's image as warrior; however, this
image again evolved in the wider context of growing English imperialism. In the
Victorian and Edwardian eras, Englishmen were encouraged to become "knights
of the empire" who would counter the threats posed both by rebels inside the
empire and by those external European nations that might try to encroach on
English territory.[16] The Black Prince became a fitting hero for these knights of
the empire; for example, in an 1852 speech, the canon of Canterbury cathedral,
Arthur Stanley, declared that the prince was a hero for soldiers fighting against
the Sikh army in India at the battles of Sobraon and Ferozeshah.[17] Elite public
schools, such as Clifton, with strong ties to the empire also made sure that
young soon-to-be knights appreciated their heroic inheritance. In 1904, when
the school erected their Boer War memorial, the Black Prince was one of the
medieval heroes chosen to grace the walls of the chapel.

To construct Edward as a national military hero on the stage of empire,
nineteenth- and early twentieth-century scholars described the prince using
terms that glorified war and emphasized the prince's martial prowess. By
choosing metaphors such as "the game," their language and rhetoric helped to
fashion Edward into a nineteenth-century sportsman warrior. Historian Robert
Williams stated that the Black Prince was a great gamesman when he played
the "rough sport" of war.[18] By using this "game" metaphor, Williams played
up the rhetoric of public school chivalry. At the same time, by emphasizing
the prince's martial prowess, historians and authors such as Douglas Sladen
and George Payne Rainsford James glorified war. In their works, war was a
game with specific rules and behaviours in which young men could perform
chivalrously and gain victory for England.[19]

By the nineteenth and early twentieth centuries, authors and historians also
began to use Edward's role as military leader to connect him more explicitly to
the different classes in England. Historians such as Cyril Robinson illustrated
that the prince's army was a national army by showcasing how members of
every class fought for the prince:

> For all their prowess and importance, the days were gone
> when this aristocracy did the whole business of fighting the
> King's battles, leaving the humbler folk to tend the sheep and
> speed the plough at home. Edward's army was no mere retinue
> of feudal lordings, trained in the pomp and etiquette of chivalry.

It was a national host: each hamlet and each borough contributed
its men.[20]

Part of this reimagining of the prince as a powerful national military hero
involved the relationship between language and audience. In the fourteenth
century, European chroniclers such as Henry Knighton, Thomas Walsingham,
the Chandos Herald, and Jean Froissart presented the prince as a noble hero
who performed for a noble audience. In his chronicles, Froissart states that
the prince spoke directly to his loyal knights before the battle of Poitiers,
encouraging them to do feats of valour.[21] After the battle, the Prince entertained
his captive, King John II of France, and praised him for his skill in battle.[22]
The fourteenth-century chronicler the Chandos Herald reinforces this vision
of the prince as a chivalrous European knight who focuses his attention after
the battle on the needs of his cousin and captive, the King of France, rather
than on the common English soldiers.[23] In the majority of fourteenth-century
chronicles, the prince rarely spoke to or acknowledged his ordinary troops.[24]
By having Edward address the nobility, fourteenth-century chroniclers and
writers imagined him as the hero of an aristocratic community.

However, not all medieval chroniclers portrayed Edward as a hero who
related primarily to the nobility. One exception was the English chronicler
Geoffrey Le Baker. In his chronicle, Le Baker had the prince address the
common soldiers before the battle of Poitiers. The prince told his men that
they should not fear the French because, in the past, Englishmen had tamed
men from all nations. The prince declared that courage is in the blood of all
Englishmen. He then linked the common soldiers to their heroic ancestors:

'Your manhood saith [Edward] hath bin always known
    to me, in great dangers, which sheweth that you are not
    degenerate from the true sonnes of English men, but to be
    descended from the blood of them which heretofore
were under my father's dukedome and his predecessors,
    kings of England.'[25]

Knights, archers, and common soldiers were joined together by their
common blood against the French. In this scene, Le Baker positioned the Black
Prince in the national community of Englishmen rather than in a transnational
and elite community of knights.[26]

In the nineteenth and early twentieth centuries, scholars such as Louise
Creighton and R.P. Dunn-Pattison focused on Le Baker as their source to link
the prince to the English people.[27] Historian Dunn-Pattison used Le Baker
extensively when he described how the prince engaged his troops before
the battle of Poitiers. According to Dunn-Pattison, the prince understood the
importance of communicating with all of his men. By speaking to the common
troops and stating that all Englishmen shared a common ancestry, the prince

was determined to make them feel a part of the English national community.[28] Louise Creighton also used Le Baker to promote an image of the prince as a man who actively engaged with his troops. In this period, nationalists used selective sources to transform the prince's image from a medieval aristocratic hero to an English gentleman warrior.

This nationalization of Edward's warrior image was most pronounced in the reinterpretation of the prince's tomb at Canterbury Cathedral. When the prince planned his tomb in the fourteenth century, he imagined a site that represented the ideals of his own European community of knights. He depicted himself as a sleeping knight in armour, a form that was easily recognizable within this transnational community.[29] European knights would have been familiar with Arthurian figures such as Sir Perceval, who freed an entombed knight, and Sir Lancelot, who slept in a forest fully clothed in his armour.[30] The prince's French epitaph appealed to the European community of knights, and it was this audience that the prince asked to pray for his entry into heaven.[31]

In the nineteenth century, however, the prince's tomb was redefined as a national monument. For Arthur Stanley, the prince's tomb was a site where Englishmen could experience their connection to the ideal character of an English gentleman hero:

> When he [Edward] died, Englishmen thought all their hopes had died with him. But we know that it was not so; we know that the life of a great nation is not bound up with the life of a single man; we know that the valour and the courtesy and the chivalry of England are not buried in the grave of the Plantagenet Prince. It needs only a glance round the country to see that the high character of an English gentleman, of which the Black Prince was the noble pattern, is still to be found everywhere.[32]

Visitors to the tomb would have been familiar with Stanley's use of the prince as a symbol of the national community, regardless of class or nobility; in the Victorian period, the monarch was consistently linked to the nation through writing and art.[33] The prince's tomb was one of many sites used by nationalists used to promote their elite vision of the English gentleman prince.

Despite its flexibility and adaptations, this image of the warrior gentleman, paragon of Victorian English identity, could not survive indefinitely. Symbolically, on May 31st 1916, the *London Times* reported that the English warship, *The Black Prince*, the pride of the Royal Navy, had been sunk during the Battle of Jutland.[34] During the Great War, the prince's public image as a warrior suffered its first blow as writers and poets began to question the gentlemanly idea of war as sport. However, the traumas of World War Two and the upheaval of decolonisation ultimately caused the downfall of the prince's Victorian and Edwardian image. The debacle at Suez in 1956 and the loss of twelve colonies from 1957-1968 made the gentlemanly ideal of English knights of the empire appear anachronistic.[35] With the loss of empire and the advent of modern warfare, the prince's image as a gentleman warrior faced its demise.

MCMASTER UNIVERSITY

NOTES

I would like to thank Dr. Gwendolyn Morgan , Montana State University, for all her valuable comments.

[1] "Leeds City Square – Unveiling the Statuary," *The Leeds and Yorkshire Mercury*, September 17, 1903: 8.

[2] Anderson, Benedict. *Imagined Communities: Reflections on the Origins and Spread of Nationalism*. 12th ed. London: Verso, 1991.

[3] Calinescu, Matei. *The Faces of Modernity*. Bloomington: Indiana UP, 1977. Pp. 3-10. Harootunian, Harry. *History's Disquiet: Modernity, Cultural Practice, and the Question of Everyday Life* New York: Columbia UP, 2000. Pp. 17-19. Berman, Marshall. *All That is Solid Melts Into Air: The Experience of Modernity*. New York: Simon and Schuster, 1982. Pp. 15-36.

[4] Collins, Arthur. *The Life and Glorious Actions of Edward Prince of Wales*. London: 1740. Pp. 74-76.

[5] Froissart, Jean. *Chronicles*. Ed. and trans. by Geoffrey Brereton. London: Penguin, 1978. P. 37.

[6] Martin, G.H. ed and trans. "Introduction." *Knighton's Chronicle* 1337-1396. Oxford: Clarendon Press, 1995. P. lxiv.

[7] Baring, Maurice. *The Black Prince and Other Poems*. London: John Lane, 1903. Pp. 31-32.

[8] Froissart 303.

[9] Colley, Linda. *Britons: Forging the Nation*. New Haven: Yale UP, 1992. Pp. 4-9, 35.

[10] Jones, Meredith. *The Story of Edward the Black Prince*. 2nd ed. London: T. Nelson and Sons, 1883. Pp. 111, 124.

[11] Jones 90, 97, 204.

[12] Sladen, Douglas B.W. *Edward the Black Prince: An Epic Drama*. 1886. London: Griffith, 1887. Pp. 74-75, 123.

[13] Froissart 59-60.

[14] Curry, Anne. *The Hundred Years War*. London: MacMillan, 1993. P. 6.

[15] Callcott, Maria. *Little Arthur's History of England*. 2nd ed. London: John Murray, 1936. Pp. 40-41. *Little Arthur's* was first published in 1835.

[16] Girouard, Mark. *The Return to Camelot: Chivalry and the English Gentleman*. New Haven: Yale UP, 1981. P. 224.

[17] Stanley, Arthur Penrhyn. "Edward the Black Prince: a lecture delivered at Canterbury Cathedral, June 1852." *Historical Monuments of Canterbury*. London: Dent, 1906. P.

155. Stanley emphasized that the prince's behavior provided a model for all citizens, not just soldiers.

[18] Williams, Robert Folkstone, esq. *Lives of the Princes of Wales: Heirs to the British Throne; with notices of the court and camp of England, from the thirteenth to the nineteenth century.* London: Henry Colburn, 1843. P. 347.

[19] Sladen 9. James, George Payne Rainsford. *A History of the Life of Edward the Black Prince.* 2 vols. London: Longman, 1836. P. 188.

[20] Robinson, Cyril E. *England: A History of British Progress from the Early Ages to the Present Day.* New York: Thomas Y. Crowell, 1928. P. 117. Robinson was born in 1884. His writing reflects the earlier Victorian and Edwardian vision of the prince.

[21] Froissart 136.

[22] Froissart 144. In medieval chronicles such as Froissart's, the prince always compliments King John even through John lost the battle of Poitiers.

[23] Chandos Herald. "Life of Edward the Black Prince." *Life and Campaigns of the Black Prince.* Ed. and trans. Richard Barber. Woodbridge: Boydell, 1979. P. 103.

[24] Ibid. P. 101.

[25] Le Baker, Geoffrey. "Chronicle." *Life and Campaigns of the Black Prince from contemporary letters, diaries and chronicles, including Chandos Herald's Life of the Black Prince.* Ed. and trans. Richard Barber. Woodbridge: Boydell, 1979. Pp. 74-78. In these speeches, Le Baker highlights the prince's ability to communicate with the common English soldier.

[26] Howard, Donald R. *Chaucer: His Life, His Works, His World.* New York: Fawcett, 1987. Pp. 21-26. During the fourteenth century, the English language was becoming more prestigious, partly as a result of authors such as Chaucer. While the language of the court was French, and French was the prince's first language, it is likely he knew enough English to carry on a conversation. His father, Edward III, was the first English monarch to speak English well.

[27] Creighton, Louise. *Life of Edward the Black Prince. Historical Biographies.* Ed. Mandell Creighton. London: Longmans, 1896. Pp. 102-103; Dunn-Pattison, R.P. *The Black Prince.* London: Methuen, 1910. P. 158.

[28] Dunn-Pattison 158.

[29] In the fourteenth century, the image of the Arthurian knight would have been familiar to European knights. For example, knights could read the *Romances of King Arthur,* which were available in England and in France, or they could read about the feats of Arthur in Geoffrey of Monmouth's *History of the King's of Britain* written in Latin, while popular cycles of Arthurian romance were available for knights to read in French. Richard Barber, *King Arthur: Hero and Legend.* Woodbridge: Boydell, 1986. Pp. 103-114; Geoffrey of Monmouth. *History of the Kings of Britain.* Trans. Lewis Thorpe. Baltimore: Penguin, 1966. Pp. 51-284.

[30] Binski, Paul. *Medieval Death: Ritual and Representation.* Ithaca: Cornell UP, 1996. P. 101; Hopkins, Andrea. *Chronicles of King Arthur.* London: Collins and Brown, 1993. Pp. 51, 74, 78, 123. Barber, Richard. *King Arthur: Hero and Legend.* Woodbridge: Boydell, 1986. Pp. 103-125.

[31] Tyson, Diana B. Tyson. "The Epitaph of Edward the Black Prince." *Medium Aevum* 46 (1977): 98-104. Edward did not write his epitaph but instead chose for his tomb a

verse from the *Disciplina Clerica*, version B, a popular poem in the fourteenth century. Harvey, John, ed. "The Poem on the Tomb of the Black Prince" *The Black Prince and His Age*. London: Batsford, 1976. Pp. 166-167. Froissart 193. According to Froissart, the European community of knight's mourned the prince's passing.

[32] Stanley 155.

[33] Cannadine, David." The Context, Performance and Meaning of Ritual: The British Monarchy and the 'Invention of Tradition', c. 1820-1977." *The Invention of Tradition*. Eds. Eric Hobsbawm and Terence Ranger. Cambridge: Cambridge UP, 2002. Pp. 101-164; Colley 210-211. Linda Colley suggests this linking of monarch and nation has its origins in the eighteenth century.

[34] "The Crews of Lost Warships. Indefatigable and Black Prince. Lists of 1,784 Names." *The Times*. June 1, 1916: 10; Amy E. Fisher, "In Memoriam H.M.S. Black Prince. *Letters to the Editor*. November 20, 1916: 3.

[35] Collins, Marcus. "The fall of the English gentleman: the national character in decline, c. 1918-1970." *Historical Research* 75 (2002): 92-93.

Small-Scale Humor in the British Medieval Revival

Clare A. Simmons

Some recent children's movies feature a phenomenon that I shall name the Mall Joke. At the movies, fairy tales almost invariably require a medieval setting, yet in a few recent fairy-tale themed movies, characters encounter a medieval shopping mall. In *Shrek 2*, Princess Fiona's parents' kingdom, the Land of Far, Far, Away, appears to be one large Disney-style mall, clearly a dig at Disney, the creators of the standard definition of what a fairy-tale land ought to be like, yet at the same time associating the concept of the mall with respectability and normal life.[1] In *Ella Enchanted*, the title character attends the royal opening of the Frell Galleria, complete with a parking lot for coaches and horses, hand-cranked wooden escalators, and shoe-racks selling glass-slippers, only to be tormented by her ugly stepsisters.[2] What is funny about medieval malls? In the first place, they allow for a tiny speck of medievalist introspection: perhaps contemporary Western society has reached the point where we cannot imagine a world without a mall, our own fairy palace of consumption. Yet we laugh, knowing that people in medieval times did not really have malls, and the twinkle of familiarity may fade into the smirk of superiority: what appears to be a point of similarity between the medieval world and ours really enforces difference.[3]

The Mall Joke, then, embodies the problem of what exactly we are laughing at. I wish to investigate whether medievalism has a sense of humor. Anyone who reads *The Canterbury Tales* is aware that people in the medieval period found things funny. Yet ever since *Don Quixote*, those of a medievalist turn have been the targets for humor. A notorious example is the Eglinton Tournament. As Mark Girouard has noted in *Chivalry and the English Gentleman*, in 1839, the thirteenth Earl of Eglinton and his aristocratic friends decided to put on a full-fledged medieval tournament, all the more impressive since the word "medievalism" had not been coined, and the *Oxford English Dictionary* records the first use of the word "mediaeval" only a generation earlier. The preparations were splendid, but as the tournament was about to begin, a violent thunderstorm washed out the proceedings and the tournament collapsed into a sea of mud.[4] Mark Girouard makes the point that when the weather finally improved, Lord Eglinton held his tournament reasonably successfully—my point here, in contrast, is that the world laughed, and that the tournament has gone down in history as an amusing medievalist disaster. From the Renaissance to the present day, for every person willing to immerse himself in the love of the medieval, be he political reformer, admirer of art or literature, or medieval re-enactor, there seem to be two or three people willing to make fun of him.

I wish to move, though, from medievalism as the subject for humor and ask whether later generations looking back on the Middle Ages can find humor in medievalism, or whether medievalism must be by definition melancholy. To return to the example of Don Quixote, at a certain point the reader may stop laughing at the self-styled knight and start to embrace his vision of a world more colorful, more selfless, and more exciting than the mundane rural society in which he lives. And when at the end of the story, the dying Quixote denounces his medievalism as madness, the reader may not agree with the narrator Cide Hamete, who states that his "desire has been no other than to cause mankind to abhor the false and foolish tales of chivalry," and wish to return into Don Quixote's dreams.[5]

For the question arises as to whether medievalism necessitates a sense of loss. Although, as *Don Quixote* proves, many earlier examples of medievalist thinking can be found, medievalism came to be identified as such in the nineteenth century, and particularly in countries such as Britain undergoing industrial, economic, and social change. Alice Chandler, in her ground-breaking book, describes nineteenth-century medievalism as a "Dream of Order."[6] The concept of a dream implies a sense of loss—a juxtaposition of past and present in which the present seems to be lacking something that the past possessed. As articulated by John Ruskin, medievalism is one of the "Trinity of Ages," of Classicalism, Mediaevalism, and Modernism. These were not for Ruskin merely styles of art, or even modes of government; they suggested to him ways of looking at the world. In *The Stones of Venice*, published in the early 1850s, Ruskin suggests that the medieval citizen was inspired by Christianity to work for the glory of God, rather than for selfish ends.[7] Medievalism thus might be a way of recapturing the corporate-minded spirit of the Middle Ages that works for a common end, yet leaves space for individual expression that modern work in an age of mass production cannot replicate. Looking back on the Middle Ages may inspire emulation, but even that emulation acknowledges the loss of medieval community. In Pugin's series *Contrasts*, the heartlessness of modern society is contrasted with the God-centered community of medieval times.[8] Some recent theorists of medievalism, such as Kathleen Biddick in *The Shock of Medievalism*, have gone so far as to suggest that medievalism is a form of desire, and must always involve some sense of loss.[9]

At the same time, there is a slightly antagonistic quality to medievalism. Leslie Workman chose for the epigraph to *Studies in Medievalism* Lord Acton's statement that "Two great principles divide the world, and contend for the mastery, antiquity and the middle ages. These are the two civilizations that have preceded us, the two elements of which ours is composed. All political as well as religious questions reduce themselves practically to this. This is the great dualism that runs through our society."[10] Medievalism constantly reminds us of opposition—between the classical and medieval heritages and values, between past and present, between ourselves and others, maybe even between Medievalism and Medieval Studies.

The twentieth century saw some humorous adaptations of the King Arthur stories, even though much of the humor in, for example, T. H. White's *The Once and Future King* and *Monty Python and the Holy Grail* is dependent on a modernist sensibility. Even the heavy hitters of twentieth-century medievalism mix comedy with mythic seriousness. A number of truly funny moments occur in C.S. Lewis's *Narnia* series—I especially like Eustace turning into a dragon in *Voyage of the Dawn Treader*—while there are a number of light-hearted scenes involving the Hobbits in *The Lord of the Rings*. One of the lines that I find the funniest actually belongs to Mr. Butterbur, the keeper of the Inn at Bree, who reacts to the shadows of the Black Riders by exclaiming, "Never has such a thing happened in my time!...Guests unable to sleep in their beds, and the good bolsters ruined and all!" Even in twentieth-century literature, however, these comic moments merely contrast with essential earnestness of the struggle between good and evil of these epic series: in fact, when Mr. Butterbur asks, "What are we all coming to?" he receives the reply, "Dark times."[11] (1:191).

To find humor in the Victorian Medieval Revival seems an even more difficult task, given that one of qualities that attracted the Victorians to the medieval period was its perceived earnestness. The Victorians are remembered more for their lack of humor than for their enjoyment of it, and Victorian theories of humor are extremely rare.[12] In 1895, William Samuel Lilley gave a series of four lectures at the Royal Institution where he attempted to define the purpose of humor. He begins by quoting W.M. Thackeray's *English Humorists of the Eighteenth Century*:

> The humourous writer proposes to awaken and direct your love, your pity, your kindness—your scorn for untruth, pretension, imposture— your tenderness for the weak, the poor, the oppressed, the unhappy. To the best of his means and ability he comments on all the ordinary actions and passions of life almost.

To this, Lilley adds, "The ordinary actions and passions of life are the subject of the humourist. But he brings to them what the Germans call *Schauen*, vision. He sees these ordinary actions and passions more clearly than we see them. . . . He pierces below the surface of things to the secret recesses of the moral world."[13] According to Lilley, then, humor is a process of defamiliarization that causes its readers or audience to interrogate their own moral assumptions.

I seek here to explore some of the small but truly medievalist ways that the Victorian Medieval Revival managed to inject some elements of humor into the model of opposition and loss that seems essential to medievalism. Humor is even harder to find in nineteenth-century medievalism than in the twentieth century. Occasional funny scenes occur in *Ivanhoe*, such as Wamba the Jester dressing up as a priest to enable Cedric to evade the clutches of the Normans. In Carlyle's Past and Present, old Abbot Hubert sets out to be healed at Canterbury, but "near Rochester City, his mule threw him, dislocated his poor kneepan, raised incurable inflammatory fever; and the poor old man got his dismissal from the whole coil at once. St. Thomas a Becket, though in a circuitous way, had *brought* deliverance!"[14] The humor here is dark indeed.[15] Burlesque plays marketed to the middle and working classes sometimes had medieval settings, but usually to provide interesting costuming for conventional romantic plots.

The true Medieval Revival, led by such serious-minded figures as Ruskin and Pugin, went so far as to create the myth of a consistently earnest, decorous Middle Ages that has in many aspects survived to the present day. These medieval enthusiasts were, at least to some degree, aware of the earthier aspects of medieval times; they just chose to ignore them. A good example is the sumptuous Kelmscott Chaucer, produced by William Morris in the 1890s and illustrated by his friend Edward Burne-Jones. It contains the entire text of Chaucer, including the bawdier stories from the Canterbury Tales. Whereas, however, the tales of courtly love and dream visions are profusely illustrated, Burne-Jones did not illustrate any of the funny stories, although perhaps one might forgive him for not etching the ending to the *Miller's Tale*.

I would suggest, though, that the widespread influence of the Medieval Revival in Britain does take a humorous form, but in works of a modest scale, usually as sketches, stories and illustrations originally produced for the rapidly expanding periodical market. An early example of this form is the *Ingoldsby Legends*, the title given to the collected stories of R.H. Barham. Barham was a school friend of the publisher Richard Bentley, and the first of the "Ingoldsby Legends" was "The Spectre of Tappington," which appeared in the February 1837 issue of *Bentley's Miscellany*.[16] The magazine had commenced publication under Charles Dickens's editorship the previous month; the February issue also contains the first installment of *Oliver Twist*. The story is headed "Fire-Side Stories:--No.1," which suggests that Barham was already planning a series. "The Spectre of Tappington," a tale of the ghostly disappearance of men's breeches, contains a number of features of later stories, including the inset story of "Bad Sir Giles" that keeps the supernatural elements in the realm of "legend;" the story-telling aspect, through, is only suggested by the title. Barham's second story, "The Legend of Hamilton Tighe," is explicitly said by Thomas Ingoldsby, the "young squire" of Tappington, to have been versified from family papers by Caroline Simpkinson.[17] In this and later contributions, which are both in prose and verse, the series title becomes "Family Stories," and by the third, "Grey Dolphin," the stories are told by different members of the household as

fireside ghost-stories. Not all of these stories are English. A famous exception
is "The Jackdaw of Rheims," the first of a number of verse tales based on
medieval legend that were nevertheless later included under the title of *The
Ingoldsby Legends*.[18] While the poems and stories are inconsistent in tone, they
display a clear affection for legends and traditions. Many of the tales are set
in the region of Tappington Hall, namely, the county of Kent, where Barham
first worked as a curate. A good example is the housekeeper's story of "The
Leech of Folkstone," in which the unfaithful wife of the owner of Marshton
Hall on Romney Marsh employs the leech to attempt to destroy her husband
by the classic magic of sticking pins in a wax effigy. He is able to thwart the
magic through the assistance of another conjurer and his black cat familiar,
who show him the plot through a magic mirror; when the conjurer attempts
to shoot the effigy, his gun blows up. Since a skeleton was found much later
with injuries that suggest it belonged to the failed conjuror, the story appears
to contain incontrovertibly supernatural elements, yet even here Mrs. Botherby
notes that "an opinion, indeed, soon prevailed, that Master Thomas Marsh had
gotten, in common parlance, exceedingly drunk on the preceding evening,
and dreamt all that he had so circumstantially related" (*Bentley's* 2:107). The
complexity of point of view allows the reader either to accept that Romney
Marsh is still in the Middle Ages, where magic still has a power, or to interpret
the story as a medievalist fantasy brought on by drink.[19]

Barham's prose and verse stories often partake of the grotesque and even
the gruesome: the ghost of Hamilton Tighe, for example, appears to those
who caused his death sitting with "his head in his lap" (*Bentley's* 1:268). "The
Nurse's Story" is an account of the magical practice of the "Hand of Glory," in
which a witch uses the hand of a man hanged for murder to make a candle
that renders the residents of Tappington Hall powerless: they are conjured to
"be as the Dead for the Dead man's sake!" (*Bentley's* 3:301). Barham's verse
moves from the horrific to the bathetic very rapidly, but often these moves
remind the reader of the mixture of ancient magic and printed record. For
example, the actual recipe is described:

'Tis awful to see
On that Old Woman's knee
The dead, shrivell'd hand, as she clasped it with glee!
And now, with care,
The five locks of hair,
From the skull of the Gentleman dangling up there,
With the grease and the fat
Of a black Tom Cat
She hastens to mix,

And to twist into wicks,
And one on the thumb, and each finger to fix.

So far, the spell appears to be from folk tradition, but the following couplet adds: "(For another receipt the same charm to prepare,/ Consult Mr. Ainsworth and *Petit Albert*):" Barham is aware that what appears to be authentically medieval is in fact medievalism.[20]

Barham makes use of Gothic typefaces and other medieval flourishes to point up his stories: in "Bloudie Jack of Shrewsberrie, The Shropshire Bluebeard," for example, the words "Bloudie Jack" are always printed in Gothic script. This use of the medieval not merely in subject-matter but also in style is developed to a far greater extent in the weekly journal *Punch*, which commenced publication about the same time. Richard Altick has discussed *Punch*'s use of the medieval as parody or pastiche.[21] Yet perhaps the *Punch* writers and illustrators, like Barham's *Ingoldsby Legends*, are not merely laughing at medievalism, but also find an inherent humor in the medieval style.

Punch commenced publication in 1841, soon after Pugin's *Contrasts* and as work continued on the solidly Gothic new Houses of Parliament. For the first few years of its publication, Punch was highly critical of the Government's failure to address serious social issues, and particularly the plight of the poor in years of agricultural distress in mainland Britain and complete disaster in Ireland. By the 1850s, *Punch* tended to associate medievalism with what it calls "Puseyism," the branch of the Anglican church that emphasized the continuity of the English church with the Roman Catholic Middle Ages. In early volumes, however, *Punch*'s use of medievalism is remarkably varied. *Punch* frequently affects to ridicule medievalism: for example, a column simply headed "The Middle Ages" from 1847 begins, "Some well-meaning people are continually talking of 'the good old times,' as if the present times were not good enough for all practical purposes. We suspect that if we could go back to the habits of our ancestors we should find them rather inconvenient..." (11:10). An article from 1850, "The Mediaeval Mania," reads, "Someone says that the history of a country is be read in its monuments: if by monuments are meant works of art; and if our history is to be read in those, we shall be treated by posterity as persons who lived in the Middle Ages, for everything around us partakes of the mediaeval character" (13:122).

Yet this medieval character strongly affected *Punch* itself. First, *Punch* began many of its columns with illuminated letter; these were often not merely a borrowing from medieval style, but featured medieval characters. In one letter, the veil descending from a woman's extraordinarily tall striped wimple looping against the back of her trailing skirt makes a really impressive "R" of "Really." In the style of medieval illuminated letters, this is both text and art, but unlike medieval art, it is signed by the artist—possibly John Doyle. (Most of the others are the work of the younger Doyle, Richard. The C of "Candles" is the tail of a dragon as a knight in a plumed helmet fights it with a lance. The D of "Doctor," which seems to portray a medieval Hamlet looking at the ghost of his father, heads a spoof of phrenology called "Stomachology" All these are in *Punch*'s very first volume, which reprinted an alphabet of illuminated letters in its index.

Richard Doyle, who contributed a series of illustrations of modern foibles titled "Manners & Customs of Ye Englyshe," was the most medievalist of the illustrators contributing to the early *Punch*, but many of the texts were also medievalist in style. The early volumes of Punch contain many, arguably too many, lays, ballads and odes written in pseudo-medieval language. For example, "Ye Hontynge of Ye Stagge," from 1846, combines many of these medievalist features. First, it is a straightforward poem telling how dogs caught and devoured an elusive stag,

> But soone dyd retrybutione juste
> > Those greedie dogges betide;
> Each one that ate ye hardie stagge
> > Of indigestchionne dyed.
>
> One onlie dogge escaped safe
> > From out that deadlie trayle,
> He was ye conynge dogge who gotte
> > Ye stagge hys tender tayle. (10:60)

There may be a reference to parliamentary in-fighting over a Bill here—could the "cunning dog" be Disraeli?—and so the text serves the dual function of pastiche and satire. The illustration portrays the hounds as lords and members of Parliament—the hound in a top hat could be Henry Brougham—but also provides a further example of *Punch*'s use of illuminated letters, both the title of the ballad and the first letter, the O of "O 'Tis merrie," being worked into the design.

Many of *Punch*'s medievalist jests come in the form of what Morton Gurewitch has called "ironic dissimulation"[22]: that is, they offer a proposal or suggestion with tongue firmly in cheek, and the reader has to use context and knowledge to recognize the ironic intention. *Punch* made a number of suggestions as to the directions that the Gothic decorations of the new Houses of Parliament might take. For example, *Punch* created a spoof of Maclise's "Spirit of Chivalry" fresco design for the House of Commons, noting, "The masterly Cartoon of MACLISE has only one fault which *Mr. Punch* feels it his duty to rectify. The error to which we allude is making the various figures in the Cartoon ideal instead of real personages....We regret, therefore, that MACLISE did not render his conception perfect by 'filling in' with portraits of the remarkable men of the present day—men with whom the pencil of *Punch* has rendered the public familiar, though the familiarity may have bred contempt in two or three instances" (9:83). We might note here *Punch*'s claim to make the faces of national figures known to the public. The figures include Peel and Stanley as the two knights flanking the Speaker of the House; Brougham as a soothsayer "who," says the text, "never says anything to soothe"; Irish nationalist Daniel O'Connell as a bard; and Disraeli as a minstrel, "playing as usual the 'precious lyre.'" As is common, Mr. Punch himself is part of the design, as, the text tells us, "the poet-historian from whom future ages must derive their knowledge of the spirit and the deeds of the chivalry of politics"—and although *Punch* may have been joking, I think history has borne out that claim. The piece is headed "*Punch*'s cartoons," which sets up a pun between "cartoon" as the design for a fresco and the "cartoon" of a comic paper—it's worth noting, though, that *Punch* reserved the word "cartoon" for the whole-page political illustrations for which it was famous, regarding the in-text illustrations as more part of the text—in fact, as illuminations in the medieval style.

Medievalism also crops up thematically. The motif of the tournament proved irresistible to *Punch*'s illustrators. Richard Doyle, who may have attended the Eglinton Tournament as a teenager with his father and drew a series of illustrations of it, was among those who enjoyed depicting political and social conflict as a battle between medieval knights. Replaying the tournament motif so beloved of nineteenth-century medievalists, some pictures represent Lord Brougham taking on the Corporation of London, and Mr. Punch himself, as the champion of the press, taking on the law and triumphing. In the title page from 1851, Mr. Punch is the king watching the tournament as the knights of Satire and Justice defeat Oppression, Twaddle, and Humbug. Medievalism here is not elitism, but a way of representing *Punch*'s championing of freedom.

Punch assumes that its readership has a reasonable familiarity with medieval English history. An early series is "Miss Tickletoby's Lectures on English History," where a schoolmistress lectures on the early history of England. Miss Tickletoby's personal view of history would not be funny if the reader did not know the standard version of the stories she relates. Of the story of Henry II's mistress Fair Rosamund, for example, Miss Tickletoby comments, "Fair Rosamund indeed! A pretty pass things are come to, when hussies like this are to be praised and bepitied!" (3:92). She tells with glee how Queen Eleanor "procured admission to the place where this saucy hussy was, and drawing from her pocket a dagger and a bowl of poison, she bad her take one or the other. She preferred, it is said, the prussic acid, and died, I have no doubts, in extreme agonies, from the effect of the draught." The illustration to Miss Tickletoby's lecture—possibly by William Makepeace Thackeray—is a grotesque sketch of an ugly Queen Eleanor offering a shrinking Rosamond the choice between poison and a dagger. Yet this illustration has a pairing in a true cartoon from the same third volume.[23] The title is "Fair Rosamond; Or, The Ashburton Treaty."[24] The figures are not in medieval costume, and so readers would need to use their knowledge of medieval legend to interpret it. The role of Queen Eleanor is taken by an emblematic representation of the United States, an Indian wearing the Stars and Stripes with the word "Slavery" around its waist; while the role of Rosamond is taken by Britannia, who chooses the poison of treaty over the dagger of war. In a gender-bending but compositionally-similar variation from a few years later, Disraeli plays the role of Rosamond, while the free-trader Richard Cobden is Eleanor, offering him—or her—the choice between the poison of Free Trade and the sword of Resignation.

The "Fair Rosamond" cartoon assumes on the part of its reader both a contemporary political awareness and a medievalist knowledge. Other early political cartoons that make use of medieval themes include Lord John Russell as King John signing Magna Carta (a failed Reform Bill, but also a reference to the Chartists, who were themselves medievalists in constructing their political demands as reviving medieval rights rather than creating new ones); and Russell as "Alfred the Small" visiting the Irish camp, an allusion to the story of Alfred the Great visiting the Danes.[25] One of the strangest examples of how these things come together, or alternatively, don't quite come together, is the way in which *Punch* chose to present Thomas Hood's poem "The Song of the Shirt." From its beginning, the poem claims a contemporary specificity:

> With fingers weary and worn,
> With eyelids heavy and red,
> A Woman sat, in unwomanly rags,
> Plying her needle and thread—
> Stitch! Stitch! Stitch!
> In poverty, hunger, and dirt,
> And still with a voice of dolorous pitch,
> She sang her Song of the Shirt!

The poem is very intense and directed in condemning the contemporary practice of piecework labor:

> O! Men, with Sisters dear!
> O! Men! with Mothers and Wives!
> It is not linen you're wearing out,

But human creatures' lives!
Stitch! Stitch! Stitch!
In poverty, hunger, and dirt,
Sewing at once, with a double thread,
A Shroud as well as a Shirt.

This would appear to have nothing to do with medievalism. Hood is highlighting a problem that Ruskin and William Morris would have argued did not exist in the Middle Ages, where, they believed, craftspeople were morally committed to the vision of what they were creating, rather than the repetitive manual labor described in Hood's poem. The poem points to a contemporary problem—yet the figures surrounding it seem medieval. Resembling the grotesques sometimes found in the borders of medieval manuscripts, a variety of figures in antiquated costume, none of whom seem to represent the woman in the poem, form a border around the text. Many have large heads and tiny bodies; a couple even appear to be ostriches in clothes. Some are leading others like animals; others perform acrobatics; a number carry whips. The usual reading of this page is that Hood's poem, apparently a late submission to *Punch*, does not fit with the illustrations drawn by Richard Doyle.[26] A closer analysis suggests, though, that the juxtaposition may have profoundly ironic resonances, while medievalism can help analyze what is happening.

In *Rabelais and His World*, Mikhail Bakhtin argues that a manifestation of medieval humor was carnival. Carnival, says Bakhtin, "sought a dynamic expression; it demanded ever changing, playful, undefined forms. All the symbols of the carnival idiom are filled with this pathos of change and renewal, with the sense of the gay relativity of prevailing truths and authorities. We find here a characteristic logic, the peculiar logic of the 'inside out,' of the 'turnabout,' of a continual shifting from top to bottom, from front to rear, of numerous parodies and travesties, humiliations, profanations, comic crownings and uncrownings."[27] In Doyle's drawings we see little dominating big, and strange struggles between odd and only partly human figures. It is difficult to analyze the individual figures—for example, across the top of page and above the poem is a small man leading a huge man like an animal while an ambiguously-gendered figure in an ermine robe seems to want to put a huge pen up its rear. Overall, though, the page partakes of the flavor of medieval carnival, under the heading "Punch's Triumphal Procession." Now, what does medieval carnival have to do with Victorian England? Often overlooked is the fact that *Punch*'s original identity was as a London paper—the subtitle is "the London Charivari," alluding to a French illustrated paper of the same name, but stressing *Punch*'s London character. "The Song of the Shirt" appeared in a several-page bordered sequence under this title of "Punch's Triumphal

Procession," and the time of year is relevant here. Towards the end of the year is not merely Christmas—a figure who may be Father Christmas appears on the right-hand margin—but also, in November, the Lord Mayor's Show. The Lord Mayor's Show is an institution that has its origins in the time of Magna Carta, when the Lord Mayor of London processes to Westminster to show his allegiance to the Crown. In Victorian England, it was both a time of officially-sanctioned pageantry and of carnivalesque celebration, one place where folk tradition met the civic establishment. The normal effect of carnival is to turn things upside-down and inside-out—but this assumes that there is a normal hierarchy and way of doing things. "The Song of the Shirt" questions normal hierarchies—if respectability of dress is dependent on degradation of one's fellow citizens, then something may be wrong with the system. Doyle's figures, some of whom seem to be making dominating or exploitative gestures towards others, might therefore seem to be asking a similar question about the status quo as does Hood's poem.

Finally, then, I would suggest that medievalist humor on a small scale may not be so incompatible with Ruskin's vision of the Middle Ages as it may at first appear. The grotesque is one of Ruskin's defining characteristics of the Gothic. Ruskin concedes that "there is jest—perpetual, careless, and not infrequently obscene—in the most noble work of the Gothic periods."[28] Ruskin distinguishes between the Northern Gothic grotesque and that of the Renaissance through the intent of the artist, the true Gothic artist possessing "the magnificent condition of fantastic imagination" (11:145), simultaneously "ludicrous and fearful" (151). The true jest, Ruskin maintains, emerges from serious thought, a reverence for the divine and for Nature, resulting in "the master of the true grotesque": "it is because the dreadfulness of the universe around him weighs upon his heart that his work is wild…" (169). Often, this will manifest itself in a form of nature—certainly true of Doyle's art in *Punch*, where people and animals often merge with vegetation. And it may also manifest itself as satire, where the simple workman mocks the failings of his social superiors (172). Although Ruskin does not explicitly make the point, it is clear from his description that the workman's scope for humorous self-expression must be a small scale, not in the cathedral as seen from afar, but in the flourishes and borders that can only be seen close up. Ruskin sees potential for both playful and earnest humor in the grotesques of the medieval cathedral, but seems to despair because in his own manufacturing age, this individual expression based on a moral consciousness of the world is no longer possible. "The Song of the Shirt" points to a huge failing in the commercial and manufacturing system of Britain during the time that was also the Medieval Revival, and I'd suggest that Doyle's illustrations, grotesque and disturbing as they are, show something of a recapturing of the medieval spirit, an opportunity to question the establishment in an artistic way. Would Ruskin have liked these drawings? I suspect not. But I would suggest that in a age of mass production, they show a way for individual craftsmanship to continue to offer a moral commentary on issues of the day, and that seems quite in keeping with Ruskin's sense of what is good about medieval artisanship.

We seem to have moved a long way from the mild self-scrutiny suggested by the "Mall joke" with which this paper began. Yet the second volume of *Punch* had its own version of the "Mall joke." A series called "Punch's Ancient Costumes" begins, "The fourteenth century is perhaps the most remarkable of all the centuries that have hitherto tumbled from the lap of Time; and its peculiar feature was probably the variety and beauty, the richness and brilliancy, the gracefulness, the warmth, the quality—in a word, the *cut* of its costumes." *Punch* claims to reproduce sketches from "an illuminated missile—or missal, as it is sometimes affectedly called—which was thrown at the head of the present Earl of Mansfield, who was then a boy at Westminster." The pictures show "The Baked Tatur Man of the Fourteenth Century," "The Pot-Boy of the Fourteenth Century," and "The Hackney Coachman of the Fourteenth Century." The joke is not particularly funny, and the series is mercifully short. But the text's awareness of medieval illumination shows *Punch* to be working in a world where there is space for medieval humor both in significant matters and in trivial ones, albeit on a small scale.

THE OHIO STATE UNIVERSITY

NOTES

[1] *Shrek 2*, directed by Andrew Adamson, Kelly Asbery, and Conrad Vernon (Dreamworks, 2004).

[2] The stepsisters are gawky rather than ugly, but they do have English accents, which in the movie fairy-tale world almost invariably denotes inner ugliness, and in this story places California-accented Ella outside their teenage mall clique. *Ella Enchanted*, directed by Tommy O'Haver (Buena Vista, 2004).

[3] The Mall Joke's humor works through incongruity and compression, two features that Sigmund Freud notes that humor has in common with dreams in *Wit and its Relation to the Unconscious*, trans. A.A. Brill (New York: Moffat, 1916). This is a rare Victorian-era study of the purposes of humor, but shares with the few British studies of humor an insistence on the essential earnestness of what appears at first consideration to be funny.

[4] Mark Girouard, *The Return to Camelot: Chivalry and the English Gentleman* (New Haven: Yale UP, 1981), 87-110.

[5] Miguel de Cervantes Saavedra, *The Ingenious Gentleman Don Quixote of La Mancha* (1605)., The Ormsby Translation, edited by Joseph R. Jones and Kenneth Douglas (New York: Norton, 1981), 830.

[6] Alice Chandler, *A Dream of Order: The Medieval Ideal in Nineteenth-Century English Literature* (Lincoln: U of Nebraska P, 1970).

[7] John Ruskin, *The Stones of Venice*, in *Works* 11:136. Subsequent references follow this edition.

[8] See A.W.N. Pugin, *Contrasts, Or, A Parallel between the Noble Edifices of the Fourteenth and Fifteenth Centuries and Similar Buildings of the Present Day; Showing the Present Decay of Taste* (London: Printed for Author, 1836).

[9] See Kathleen Biddick, *The Shock of Medievalism* (Durham: Duke UP, 1998).

[10] *Studies in Medievalism*, Edited by Leslie Workman, Kathleen Verduin, Thomas Shippey, et al, Title page.

[11] J. R.R. Tolkien, *The Lord of the Rings* (1955; New York: Quality Paperbacks, 1995) 1:119.

[12] A subject search of The Ohio State University Library produced no results for "Victorian humor." Excluding works on comic drama, the Victorians seem to have written few studies of humor, in contrast with the large number of American works on "wit and humor" of the later nineteenth century. Even in the United States, though, periodical literature was one of the major outlets for humorous writing.

[13] William Samuel Lilly, *Four English Humourists* (London: John Murray, 1895), 3-4.

[14] Thomas Carlyle, *Past and Present*. Ed. Richard D. Altick (New York: New York UP, 1965), 67.

[15] Carlyle is one of the "Four English Humorists" of W.S. Lilley's 1895 lecture series (the others are the generally anti-medievalist Dickens and Thackeray, and, oddly, George Eliot). Lilly calls Carlyle "intensely human," and thus "faults and foibles incident to humanity came out in him more strongly than they are wont to come out in more animal men" 120-21.

[16] R. H. Barham, "The Spectre of Tappington," *Bentley's Miscellany* 1 (February 1837): 191-207. Subsequent references cite *Bentley's Miscellany* by volume and page-number unless otherwise specified.

[17] Barham drops the reference to Caroline's part in the collected edition, where more of the pieces are described as "legends": for example, "Aunt Fanny—The Tale of a Shirt" becomes "Aunt Fanny—The Legend of a Shirt."

[18] Besides pieces ascribed simply to "Thomas Ingoldsby," Barham had three series in *Bentley's Miscellany*: "Fireside Tales," "Golden Legends" (that draw on his research in medieval sources), and "County Legends." The third is significant because it is bringing the concept of "legend" into England.

[19] Legal definitions of witchcraft are mainly post-medieval; in the nineteenth century, however, witchcraft and magic often mark "difference" between the medieval and modern world.

[20] Barham was later to work with Ainsworth when Ainsworth succeeded Dickens as the editor of *Bentley's*.

[21] Richard D. Altick, *Punch: The Lively Youth of a British Institution, 1841-1851* (Columbus: Ohio State UP, 1997) 116-118.

[22] Morton Gurewitch, *The Ironic Temper and the Comic Imagination* (Detroit: Wayne State UP, 1994), 12.

[23] *Punch* reserved the term "cartoon" for its full-page political illustrations. Often, these were planned by the editorial board and then assigned to artists such as John Tenniell, best-remembered for his illustrations to another work with sly medievalist references, *Alice's Adventures in Wonderland*. In effect, the editors regarded the smaller engravings as integral to the text, and like medieval illuminators, saw text and illustration as working closely together.

[24] The Ashburton Treaty established the border between New Brunswick and Maine.

[25] *Punch* 14:221 and 15:122. Although *Punch*'s general politics are still reformist at this time, there is apparent disapproval of Russell's flirtation both with broadening the electorate and with Irish Home Rule; both these political initiatives were to lead to nothing.

[26] See, for example, Altick, 157.

[27] Mikhail Bakhtin, *Rabelais and His World*, trans. Helene Iswolsky (Cambridge, MA: M.I.T. Press, 1968), 11.

[28] John Ruskin, *The Stones of Venice*, in *Works* 11:136.

"The Monsters Do Not Depart": Re-Unifying Norse, Anglo-Saxon, and Christian in Tolkien's *Lord of the Rings*

Brian C. Johnsrud

"Let us by all means esteem the old heroes: men caught in the chains of circumstance or of their own character, torn between duties equally sacred, dying with their backs to the wall"

~ J.R.R. Tolkien in "Beowulf: The Monsters and the Critics"

J.R.R. Tolkien saw something fundamentally lacking in the 20th century populous. While other authors such as T.S. Eliot focused on the lack of heroic opportunity for the prototypical man, J.R.R. Tolkien despaired in the lack of heroism *within* men. Caught in an age of heroic disillusionment (himself a soldier in WWI and his son, Christopher, drafted in WWII), Tolkien sought a true heroic ideal, which his studies in Anglo-Saxon literature offered. The valor of Byrhtwold, munificence of Byrhtnoth, and courage of Beowulf unquestionably inspired Tolkien. When creating Middle-earth, these admirable traits were essential in creating a new mythology for England. However, the Anglo-Saxons that Tolkien admired were separated from him in a profound way: they had no sense of divine intervention or mythology. By the time the Anglo-Saxons entered England, they had abandoned any significant or organized worship of gods or higher powers, carrying with them half-forgotten names of rejected gods. Thus, Tolkien re-created Anglo-Saxon heritage, linking their ancestry and mythological background to their Scandinavian "cousins." Furthermore, he introduced Christianity to the Northern "theory of courage," and—unlike in documented history—the combination in Middle-earth is seamless.

Unfortunately for Tolkien, the well of native English mythology is remarkably dry, an obstacle when drawing on older stories to create his national myth. In his letters he comments, "I was from early days grieved by the poverty of my own beloved country: it had no stories of its own (bound up with its tongue and soil), not of the quality that I sought, and found (as an ingredient) in legends of other lands" (*Letters* 144). The Anglo-Saxons, his favorite English ancestors, left him with scarce historical remains of any organized religion. For instance, there are no structural remains of any pagan temples from Anglo-Saxon England, though it is plausible that if any had existed, they were converted to Christian purposes by Augustine and his successors (Blair 121). There was certainly rudimentary worship, considering the existing place names containing *hearh*, meaning 'hill sanctuary,' *weoh* 'idol' or 'shrine,' and *ealh* 'temple.' Beyond that, Peter H. Blair, building off Margaret Gelling's,

"Further Thoughts on Pagan Place-Names," points out that the few references to Anglo-Saxon deities exist now solely in place names:

> The names of Thunor and Woden are found as the first element in a considerable number of place-names....Such names as Thursley, Thunderfield, Thundersley, Thurstable and many others attest the worship of Thunor....Names such as Woodnesborough, Wednesbury, Wednesfield, and many others similarly attest the cult of Woden. (Blair 123-4)

However, these scarce references confirm no uniformity in belief or practice, as they are entirely absent from southwest England and everything north of Humber (Blair points to British Christianity's influence as a likely cause).

Either way, cults associated with Thunor or Woden were extremely localized, leaving no traces of ecclesiastical hierarchy, regulation of beliefs, or even collective worship of similar gods within small tribes. Burial customs, for instance, show remarkable variation between regions: "bodies could be cremated or buried, with or without elaborate furnishings of grave goods" (Fisher 65). In spite of this deficiency of a pantheon proper, *Beowulf* and other Anglo-Saxon texts do illustrate a more universal "higher power": Wyrd. This indifferent force, nonetheless, can hardly be considered a divine aid. In *Beowulf*, the famous prince of the Geats advises, "Often, for undaunted courage/ [Wyrd] spares the man it has not already marked" (*Beowulf* 572-3, original text in brackets). However apathetically Wyrd may "mark" a man, Beowulf implies that this may be overlooked in the event of "undaunted courage." This attitude, which Tolkien later terms the Northern "theory of courage," is an exceedingly rare cultural attribute. The Romans who occupied England, for instance, embraced a pantheon of gods and goddesses to inspire their troops. However, the ideal Roman hero was markedly different from a character like Birhtnoth, memorialized in *The Battle of Maldon*. The Romans experienced an intricate balance of the intelligence and strategy of Minerva with the strength and stamina of Mars. The military precision of a Roman soldier was calculated and systematic, and demanded success. This is hardly comparable to Birhtnoth rashly abandoning logic by offering opposing Viking forces a physical advantage. Moreover, where a Roman soldier would anticipate defeat and organize a retreat, Byrhtnoth disregards any hope of success and confronts certain doom. Such comparisons are applicable to virtually every warrior culture with possible influence on the Anglo-Saxons. Without doubt, the Nordic warriors referred to in epics such as the *Prose Edda* and the *Kalevala* are the only logical "relatives" to the English heroes of *The Battle of Maldon*.

Furthermore, Northern literature provides something the Anglo-Saxon canon does not: a catalogue of gods to encourage heroic action. Unlike

Christianity, Northern heroism offered no eternal reward other than fame and glory in a bard's tale. Obviously, Tolkien was attracted to such potent conviction, especially when reflected in English literature. Tom Shippey, one of the few scholars to examine Tolkien's fascination with the Northern "theory of courage," points out that:

> In a sense this Northern mythology asks more of people than Christianity does, for it offers them no heaven, no salvation, no reward for virtue except the somber satisfaction of having done right....Tolkien wanted his characters in *The Lord of the Rings* to live up to the same high standard. (*Author of the Century* 150)

Yet, can a theoretical concept of "courage" justify a cultural cognate between Nordic and Anglo-Saxon culture? Shippey breaks comparative mythologists who treat Tolkien's work into two groups: those who assume a hereditary connection between these two cultures, and others who insist that Anglo-Saxons "were really rather *like* the Norse, so that you can argue back from the one to the other. Sometimes Tolkien took the latter route" (*Road to Middle-earth* 305). Either way, before including Norse myth into his recipe for a created English mythology, Tolkien would have to justify the validity of Norse influence—were their beliefs simply forced onto England with Viking invasion, or does Northern mythology have a more ancient claim to English history?

Actually, there is evidence of Scandinavian interaction with England even before the Anglo-Saxon migration. Norwegian graves have revealed sets of scales and weights borrowed from the system of weights in Imperial Rome (Blair 56). What's more, England was within Scandinavia's reach long before Viking attacks. Shippey notes Tolkien's mixed feelings regarding Old Norse influence: "Tolkien never lost this ambiguity about the Old Norse heathen tradition, as one can see from his maneuverings between English and Norse ascriptions on 'The Homecoming of Beorhtnoth'" (*Road* 306). These interactions, however legitimizing of Scandinavia's claim to English history, were far too brief to include any sort of religious "conversion" of England. Rather, the only tribes to bring legendary heroes such as Beowulf were those who later became the Anglo-Saxons.

Taking this into account, Tolkien had to rely on—or create—the possibility of a greater Germanic tribe from which Northern men and Anglo-Saxons both originated. In reference to a native heroic relation, Tolkien suggests, "the fundamentally similar heroic temper of ancient England and Scandinavia cannot have been founded on (or perhaps rather, cannot have generated) mythologies divergent on this essential point" (*Monsters* 21). Tolkien's theory is not singular—Brian Bates, for instance, indicates that "[t]he Norse invaders were originally from the same ethnic stock as the Anglo-Saxons, and much of their culture was the same" (29). In actuality, these two cultures both emphasized the importance of a mythologically based heritage. Bates argues that:

> In early European and Norse tribal cultures people identified with their ancestors, and leaders in particular would name a long personal heritage, going back many generations. Ultimately, the chieftains claimed their earliest ancestor as the god Woden (called Odin in the Norse culture). This sacred heritage filled them with 'mania' or life-force. (12)

Surprisingly, while the Anglo-Saxons leave no solid traces of *worshiping* Germanic deities, they relied on these ancient powers to validate their gallantry—in the eighth century, Bede legitimizes Horsa's ancestral link to Woden. Additionally, around the same time St. Boniface records the continental Saxons saying of the English, "we are of one and the same blood and bone," underscoring their consciousness of cultural history and lineage (29).

Norse tradition, without a doubt, has roots in an earlier Germanic tradition. The two shared common burial and fertility rights along with cognate gods Tiw, Odin (Woden), Thor and Frey (Freyja) (Loyn 3-4). However, the ancestral link between *Scandinavian* and *Anglo-Saxon* tribes is certainly an intriguing one. During the migration to England, the Anglo-Saxons clearly lost most of the deities that their Scandinavian relatives retained. Yet, even Shippey postulates that Tolkien may have questioned the extent to which this was true: "Maybe the Anglo-Saxons *before they migrated to England* were different. What would have happened had they turned East, not West, to the German plains and the steppes beyond?" (*Road* 126).

Invented or authentic, historical accuracy was incredibly important to Tolkien's vision of Middle-earth. Therefore, it was not enough to mimic the Anglo-Saxon "theory of courage"—its roots had to be unearthed. And, as a devout Catholic, Tolkien insisted that the *inspired* heroism of the Anglo-Saxons, entirely forgotten in modern England, must have roots in an older religious pantheon. For Tolkien, these quests for lineage—proper or invented—inexorably lead him back to the Norse tradition. If Middle-earth was to be a true saving mythology for England, it had to reflect Anglo-Saxon heroism *and* the ancient Norse pantheon, while also allowing for his Christian beliefs to co-exist. The combination of these attributes infuses god-inspired courage in the heroes of Middle-earth, even after the "powers" have departed.

Luckily, the nature of the Norse gods makes them adaptable, unpredictable, and even replaceable. The malleability of the Scandinavian heroic spirit can be traced to a unique element of Norse mythology that separates it from other European myths. The Germanic gods were mitigated and otherwise adversely affected by the migration to Scandinavia. Henry Loyn attributes this transformation to the harsh survival conditions of the Northern men, creating "a curious attitude of equality towards the gods. The Scandinavian did not creep to the alter. The gods themselves were subject to testing and open to rejection if a stronger deity than they appeared" (4). Verily, the Norse gods are *fated* to mortality. In accordance with Ragnarök, the great equalizer between men and the gods, the Norse pantheon is destined to die. Tolkien further outlines Norse provisional divinity during Ragnarök—perhaps his explanation of the absentee deities in Anglo-Saxon England. In the last battle, Tolkien illuminates the inherent good in mankind, as the gods invite mortals to battle against the monsters of the earth,

> Men are their chosen allies, able when heroic to share in this 'absolute resistance, perfect because without hope'. At lease in this vision of the final defeat of the humane (and of the divine made in its image), and in the essential hostility of the gods and heroes on the one hand and the monsters on the other, we may suppose that pagan English and Norse imagination agreed. (*Monsters* 21)

Interestingly, with such a feeble collection of gods, the Anglo-Saxons were uninterested with apocalypse. While comparing Ragnarök to the Anglo-Saxon world view, Patrick Curry points out, "Ragnarök was a relatively late aspect of German-Scandinavian mythology that never caught on in the pagan Anglo-Saxon England that so influenced Tolkien. Even then, it was, apparently, un-English in its melodrama" (Curry 48). Tolkien speculates that, although the pagan English did not embrace Ragnarök as their own, along with the modern English they had the *potential* to welcome the heroic spirit of "absolute resistance, perfect because without hope." Tolkien underscores this oddity in Norse mythology by observing, "…we may with some truth contrast the 'inhumanness' of the Greek gods, however anthropomorphic, with the 'humanness' of the Northern, however titanic" (*Monsters* 25). When the barrier between mortal and immortal fades, the gods become more human and, in turn, humans become more divine.

Eventually, the ill-fated Norse gods fall; in spite of that, traces of divinity remain in heroes like Beowulf, as Tolkien insists "the mighty ancestors of northern kings (English and Scandinavian)…had become in their very being the enlarged shadows of great men and warriors upon the walls of the world" (*Monsters* 25). An internalization of self-reliance transpires, with the acceptance that divine powers have "faded." Beowulf loosely mentions Wyrd's intervention and instead trusts his native courage and skill. Tolkien suggests, "[t]he [Norse] gods faded or receded, and man was left to carry on his war unaided. His trust was in his own power and will, and his reward was the praise of his peers during his life and after his death" (36). The beauty of Beowulf's final battle with the dragon is the utter hopelessness—it is assured to be Beowulf's end, yet he still fights. Similarly, before the Battle of Pelennor Fields Théoden tells his men, "Foes and fire are before you, and your homes far behind. Yet, though you fight upon an alien field, the glory that you reap there shall be your own for ever" and, upon his death, proclaims, "I felled the black serpent. A grim morn, a glad day, and a golden sunset!" (*Return of the King* 818, 824). Théoden, more so than any other of Tolkien's character, is the embodiment of Beowulf's fierce courage *in spite of* assured defeat. When contending with the "theory of courage," hope is irrelevant; as Shippey explains, "Tolkien knew that in the Norse mythology Von, Hope, is not one of the three cardinal virtues but, contemptuously, the drool that runs from the mouth of Fenris-Wolf" (*Author* 153).

In this way, Tolkien's potentially obscure concept of "heroic spirit" has lasted centuries. He insists that, "[o]f pagan 'belief' we have little or nothing left in English. But the spirit survived. Thus the author of *Beowulf* grasped fully the idea of *lof* or *dom*, the noble pagan's desire for the *merited praise* of the noble" (*Monsters* 36). Still, in re-inventing a lineage for this courageous spirit, and thereby adopting a historical migration of Germanic religious beliefs, what happens when a devout Catholic such as Tolkien decides to place brutal, pagan gods alongside Christ in England's created mythology? Tolkien was well acquainted with this medieval literary phenomenon. As Christianity surfaces in England, the country's frail bonds with Norse mythology are never entirely broken, but instead they are twisted and knotted with other beliefs. While the native tradition calls for bold, hopeless action, the Christianity brought to England advocates a Christian hero who reluctantly submits to his enemy. When these two radically different interpretations of courage collide, the combination is virtually comic. A fitting example is *The Dream of the Rood* and its depiction of an almost warrior-like Jesus: "Then the young hero stripped himself—that was God Almighty—strong and stouthearted" (27). When analyzing similarly conflicting elements in *Beowulf,* Tolkien appreciates the difficulty the medieval English had in keeping "Scandinavian bogies and the Scriptures separate in their puzzled brains" (*Monsters* 19). This bemusement was especially problematic for Christian devotees during England's conversion when throughout north-western England, "sculptured stone crosses…portray scenes from Scandinavian mythology….the form of the monuments themselves is likewise testimony that those who set them up were in their own eyes Christians" (Blair 167).

If Middle-earth was to harbor pagan and Christian traditions alike, it would have to be done in a different, more theologically sound manner. Luckily, Tolkien was not averse to theologically *and* academically considering the merit of medieval paganism. After Tolkien converted his long-term friend, C.S. Lewis, to Catholicism, neither lost their interest in all things pagan as Lewis afterwards attested: "If Christianity is only a mythology, then I find the mythology I believe in is not the one I like best. I like Greek mythology much better: Irish better still: Norse best of all" (Lewis 152). Besides showing the common interests between these friends, this statement is especially revealing with regard to their ability to examine modern religion as myth and vice-versa. In one of his letters, Tolkien attests, "I believe that legends and myth are largely made of 'truth'…and long ago certain truths and modes of this kind were discovered and must always reappear" (*Letters* 147).

Developing possible approaches to the fusion of pagan and Christian, Tolkien exemplifies the heroic tradition displayed as Beowulf defeats the dragon. While the Bible, specifically Revelation, references dragons, the tradition of *heroes fighting dragons* is undeniably Germanic and Scandinavian. In fact, Tolkien goes to great lengths to solidify this Norse characteristic and prove that Beowulf's admirable status as a dragon-slayer could only originate in the north,

> As for the dragon: as far as we know anything about these old poets, we know this: the prince of the heroes of the North…was a dragon slayer. And his most renowned deed…was the slaying of the prince of legendary worms. Although there is plainly considerable difference between the later Norse and the ancient English form of the story alluded to in *Beowulf,* already there it had these two primary features: the dragon, and the slaying of him as the chief deed of the greatest heroes. (*Monsters* 16)

Truly, what greater last deed could a hero who embodies Northern heroism ask for than the infamous slaying of a dragon? Yet, in the process of Christian interpolations, Tolkien insists, "Beowulf's dragon, if one wishes really to criticize, is not to be blamed for being a dragon, but rather for not being dragon enough, plain pure fairy-story dragon" (17). While the Christian audience may be astounded by its bold presence, the Northern heroes would quite likely find the dragon lacking and even unfamiliar.

Despite previous failures to unite seamlessly pagan heroism and Christianity, Tolkien recognizes that the sometimes-abrupt synthesis of the two eventually balances their beliefs, for "[i]t would seem to have been part of the English temper in its strong sense of tradition…that it should…preserve much from the northern past to blend with southern learning, and new faith" (23-24). Tolkien found that simply dealing with Germanic myths is problematic, considering their corruption. Probably raised by its revival during WWII, the issue of English vs. German heritage became supremely relevant to Tolkien. He wrote to his son, Michael, explaining his disdain of the current English prejudice against all things "Germanic":

> I have spent most of my life…studying Germanic matters (in the general sense that includes England and Scandinavia). There is a great deal more force (and truth) than ignorant people imagine in the 'Germanic' ideal. [Hitler was involved in r]uining, perverting, misapplying, and making for ever accursed, that noble northern spirit, a supreme contribution to Europe, which I have ever loved, and tried to present in its true light. Nowhere, incidentally, was it nobler than in England, nor more early sanctified and Christianized. (*Letters* 55-56)

With this pressure in mind, Tolkien tirelessly sculpted his representations of Anglo-Saxon culture in *The Lord of the Rings*. Like the *Beowulf*-poet, Tolkien veiled the Rohirrim's Christianity by merely leaving them void of any paganism: they "did not worship pagan gods; they did not hold slaves, commit incest, practice polygamy ….They are so virtuous that one can hardly call them pagans at all" (*Road* 202). In the same way, no inhabitant of Middle-earth is given specifically Christian attributes as much as they are stripped of any pagan traits—except heroics, of course.

The men of Middle-earth, however, are quite secondary when considering *The Silmarillion*. In fact, thousands of years pass before men "awake," and Middle-earth is populated by elves, dwarves, and an interesting blend of "powers." Shippey believes that "Tolkien had done his best to root his *Silmarillion* story in what little genuine Anglo-Saxon tradition he could find" (*Road* 307). It would be more accurate, perhaps, to say that the story is rooted in the Anglo-Saxon *loss of tradition*. The tale, in the first few pages, ingeniously solves the pagan/Christian gods dilemma. First, the revival of the Norse tradition brought with it all of the moral deprivation which Tolkien was forced to edit: "It is not just slaughter, trickery, deception, and indifference to another's pain that mark most of these Northern deities but *delight* in slaughter, *pride* in trickery or deceit" (Burns 166). When creating the Valar, Tolkien had no qualms with editing out any blemishes that besmirched the original deities. While his final editing left many of the Norse gods almost unrecognizable (due in part to the blending of other mythologies), the final product is a pantheon where, "with the exception of Melkor, there is no excess, no cruelty, no evil of any kind" (175).

The essential characteristic of the Valar, mimicking Norse deities, is their ultimately futile relationship to man. Tolkien stressed that "the Children of God were not under [the Valar's] ultimate jurisdiction: they were not allowed to destroy them, or coerce them with any 'divine' display of the powers they held over the physical world" (*Letters* 206). The Valar are, in all ways, subject to Eru and, as time progresses, less relevant to the world of men. Therefore, with the re-vamped Scandinavian gods to guide the creation of Arda, from the beginning of *The Silmarillion* Arda is filled with marvelously courageous, heroic, and *Norse* characters—until the time comes for them to depart and for men inherit their courageous tradition.

Above the minor pantheon of Norse gods, Tolkien seamlessly wove in an "All-Father" Christian god: Ilúvatar, or Eru. Ilúvatar is the omnipotent, omniscient, omnipresent architect of Middle-earth. He designs Middle-earth; the Valar build it by singing it into existence. Marjorie Burns comments, "[m]uch will change over the years, as Tolkien revises his myth, but not this image of Eru as "The One" (166). Indeed, throughout *The Silmarillion*, the authority of Manwë has nothing to do with *his* power, but rather his function as a communicator with the greater, singular God. When commenting on the marvelous solution to the medieval conundrum that plagued Tolkien (the loss of *admirable* traits when pagan and Christian fused), Burns points out, "[b]y sharing out the godhead role into two differing forms, Tolkien was able to evoke the ancient world and still satisfy the religious beliefs of the modern one" (176).

The Anglo-Saxon *loss of tradition* is re-created in Middle-earth as the men of Númenor step beyond their limits and try to approach Aman. Much like the Scandinavian warriors, they consider the "powers" challengeable. However, their Northern spirit proves to be more foolish than courageous. The moment they approach on Aman, a cosmic split disaffiliates the Undying Lands—along with the deities who abide there—from the physical realm of Arda: "the world was diminished, for Valinor and Eressëa were taken from it into the realm of hidden things" (*Silmarillion* 334-5). If the Númenóreans are viewed as Tolkien's image of the ancient Germanic origin, then the god-challenging Númenóreans are clearly the Scandinavian offshoot. However, some Númenóreans refused to fight, and instead, like the migrating Anglo-Saxons, voyaged to a foreign land without their native gods. Regarding the historical shift towards the dominance of men, Tolkien writes, "[a]s the stories become less mythical, and more like stories and romances, Men are interwoven" (*Letters* 149). As evidence, only vague hints of the "powers" remain in later ages of Middle-earth—consider the sporadic invocations of Elbereth in *The Lord of the Rings*. In a letter concerning the religious practices of these Númenórean descendents, Tolkien explains that:

> When the 'Kings' came to an end there was no equivalent to a 'priesthood': the two being identical in Númenórean ideas. So while God (Eru) was a datum of good Númenórean philosophy, and a prime fact in their conception of history, He had at the time of the War of the Ring no worship and no hallowed place....They had (I imagine) no

petitionary prayers to God; but preserved the vestige of thanksgiving. (*Letters* 206)

This cultural description is amazingly similar to the historical accounts of the religious practices of Anglo-Saxon England. And, as Tolkien intended, the Númenórean descendents are given vague features of Christianity—prayers of thanksgiving, after all, are placed before petition in Catholicism.

Hence, Tolkien's need to establish Anglo-Saxon spiritual heritage becomes clear; the fate of the Númenóreans is inextricably linked to Anglo-Saxon English history. Both migrated and were separated by their "powers;" however, both anticipate a promising future:

It is to be presumed that with the reemergence of the lineal priest kings (of whom Lúthien the Blessed Elf-maiden was a foremother) the worship of God would be renewed, and His Name (or title) be again more often heard. But there would be no *temple* of the True God while Númenorean influence lasted. (*Letters* 207)

Anglo-Saxons and Númenóreans both ultimately await a time when justice will be restored along with the faith of the "All-Father," and until then they rely on their native heroic temperament to sustain them.

The year before his death, Tolkien wrote in a letter to his son, Christopher, "I shall never write any ordered biography—it is against my nature, which expresses itself about things deepest felt in tales and myths" (*Letters* 420-421). Hence, aside from intimations and explanations in his letters, Tolkien's sincere conviction regarding England and its mythological history lies in his creative work. Of course, any biographical study of Tolkien reveals the unfortunately troubled age he lived in. While the rest of the world looked forward, hoping for an answer from industrial advancement, Tolkien retreated to the past to uncover what should never have been lost from our world – heroes. But, by creating his *own* world, "should never have been" is easily changed to "never was." Even though the Norse gods faded from the memory of medieval England, their memory remained in the Anglo-Saxon heroic tradition; although the Valar slipped away from Arda, their spirit lingers in the bloodlines of Middle-earth. In *Beowulf,* a part of the ancestral majesty of dragons may have diminished, but in *The Hobbit,* a clever, horrific, and Norse-worthy dragon still plagues the lake-town Esgaroth: "...the northern has power, as it were, to revive its spirit even in our own times. It can work, even as it did work with the *goðlauss* Viking, without gods...for the monsters do not depart, whether the gods go or come" (*Monsters* 22-26).

MONTANA STATE UNIVERSITY

WORKS CITED

Bates, Brian. *The Real Middle-Earth*. New York: Palgrave Macmillan, 2002.

Beowulf. Trans. Seamus Heaney. New York: W.W. Norton & Company, 2000.

Blair, Peter Hunter. *An Introduction to Anglo-Saxon England*. Cambridge: Cambridge UP, 2003.

Burns, Marjorie J. "Norse and Christian Gods: The Integrative Theology of J.R.R. Tolkien." In *Tolkien and the Invention of Myth*. Ed. Jane Chance. Lexington: UP of Kentucky, 2004.

Curry, Patrick. *Defending Middle-Earth: Tolkien, Myth, and Modernity*. Edinburgh: Floris Books, 1997.

"The Dream of the Rood." Trans. E.T. Donaldson. *The Norton Anthology of English Literature*.

   Ed. M.H. Abrams. New York: W.W. Norton & Company, 2000.

Lewis, C.S. *They Asked for a Paper: Paper and Addresses*. London: Bles, 1962.

Loyn, Henry. *The Vikings in Britain*. Cambridge: Blackwell Publishers, 1994.

Shippey, Tom. *The Road to Middle-Earth*. New York: Houghton Mifflin, 2003.

_____. *Author of the Century*. New York: Houghton Mifflin, 2002.

Tolkien, J.R.R. "Beowulf: The Monsters and the Critics." In *Tolkien: The Monsters and the Critics and Other Essays*. Ed. Christopher Tolkien. London: George Allen and Unwin, 1997.

_____. *The Letters of J. R. R. Tolkien*. Ed. Humphrey Carpenter. Boston: Houghton Mifflin, 1981.

_____. *The Return of the* King. Boston: Houghton Mifflin, 1994.

_____. *The Silmarillion*. Ed. Christopher Tolkien. New York: Ballantine Books, 1997.

J.R.R. Tolkien and Walther von der Vogelweide:
Faerie and Reality

Jaimie Hensley

Original Text

Owê war sint verswunden   alliu mîniu jâr!
ist mir mîn leben getroumet   oder ist ez wâr?
daz ich ie wânde daz iht   wære, waz daz iht?
dar nâch hân ich geslâfen   und enweiz es niht.
nû bin ich erwachet,   und ist mir unbekant
daz mir hie vor was kündic   als mîn ander hant.

liut unde lant da ich von   kinda bin erzogen,
die sint mir frömde worden   reht als ez sî gelogen.
die mîne gespilen wâren   die sint træge unt alt.
verœset ist daz velt,   verhouwen stât der walt:
wan daz daz wazzer fliuzet   als ez wilent flôz,
für wâr ich wânde mîn   unglücke wurde grôz.

mich grüezet maneger trâge,   der mich bekande ê
      wol.
diu welt ist allenthalben   ungenâden vol.
als ich gedenka an manegen   wünneclîchen tac,
die mir sint enphallen   gar als in daz mêr ein slac,
iemer mêr ouwê.

Modern German

O weh, wohin sind alle meine Jahre verschwunden!
Habe ich mein Leben geträumt, oder ist es wahr?
Was ich immer glaubte, es sei, war das etwas?
So habe ich geschlafen und weiß nichts davon.
Nun bin ich erwacht und ist mir unbekannt,
was mir einst wie meine Hand vertraut gewesen.

Land und Leute, wo ich aufgewachsen bin,
die sind mir fremd geworden wie eine Lüge.
Die meine Gespielen waren, die sind träge und alt.
Verödet ist das Feld, zerstört ist der Wald:

wenn nicht das wasser flösse, wie es ehdem floß,
fürwahr, ich würde meinen, mein Unglück sei groß
  geworden.

Mich grüßt mancher säumig, der mich einst wohl
  kannte.
Die Welt ist allenthalben voll Mißgunst.
So denke ich an manchen freudenvollen Tag,
der mir entfallen ist ganz wie ein Schlag ins Meer,
für immer, o weh!

English
O woe, whither have all my years disappeared!
Is my life dreamed, or is it true?
What I always believed it were, was that (even) anything?
So (or: "in such a way") have I slept and know nothing thereof.
Now have I awakened and unknown to me is what once had been as
  familiar as my hand.

People and land where I from childhood was raised—they have become
  strange to me like a lie. (or: "as if they were lied").
Those who were my playmates—they are lazy/inert and old.
Desolate has the field become, destroyed is the forest:
If this water were not flowing as it flowed long ago,
forsooth, I would believe: my misfortune/misery would have become great.

Dully some greet me, some who once knew me well.
The world is everywhere full of ill will.
So I think of many a joy-filled day
That has slipped from me much like a surge in the sea,
forever(more), o woe!

—Walther von der Vogelweide, 1170(?)—1228(?)

From the disappearance of time to the hostility of a once-familiar land,
the above excerpt from Walther von der Vogelweide's poem exhibits many
elements of the theories and themes behind J.R.R. Tolkien's works. In fact,
the connection is undeniable. Many works of the twelfth-century Minnesänger
and poet involve the same theoretical foundations found in Tolkien's fiction
and scholarly pieces.

The existence of Primary Reality and Faerie, or an invented, secondary reality[1], is prominent in Tolkien's works. Between these two realms are many "bridges" that can bring one to and from each realm. Time, memory, and dreams serve as perhaps the most common vehicles. However, the sea seems to have been a bridge between the two worlds. And both the sea and Christianity serve as vehicles to the afterlife as well, which may or may not be connected to Faerie.

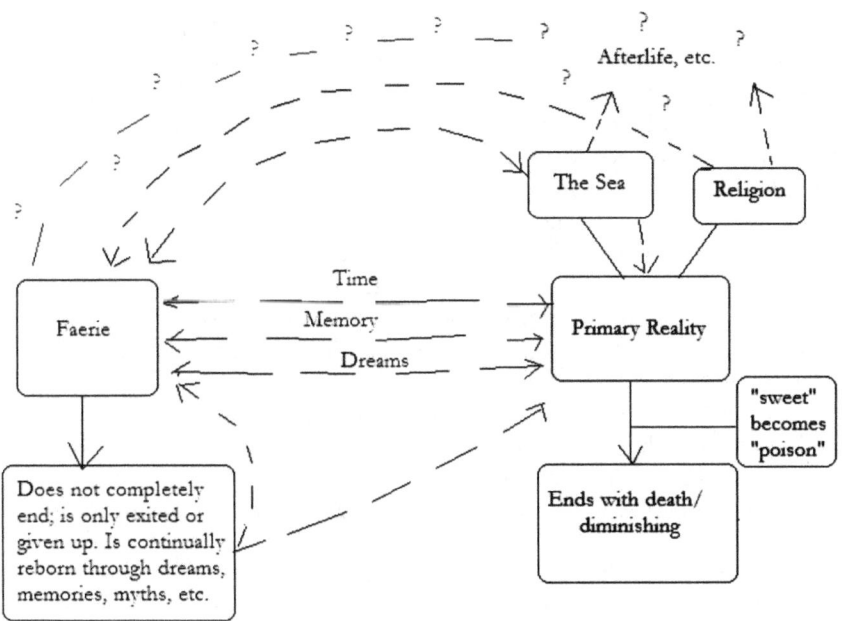

Figure 1

The above figure is by no means near exhaustive, but it serves an important purpose: each element is found not only in Tolkien's work, but also in the work of Walther von der Vogelweide, who wrote some seven-hundred years earlier. Tolkien himself speculated about "the Cauldron of Story" ("On Fairy Stories" 125) in which elements, themes, characters, quests—everything that goes into a story—boil, "waiting for the great figures of Myth and History, and for the yet nameless He or She, waiting for the moment when they are cast into the simmering stew" (127) to be mixed together into a new (if anything can be called "new") story. And the poetry of Walther von der Vogelweide heartily seasons Tolkien's stew.

Primary Reality

To better understand this complex system that runs in the background of Tolkien's writings, one must examine each part in detail. Primary Reality seems a logical place to start. One of the most recurrent aspects of Tolkien's world in the Primary Reality is that everyone and everything must diminish and eventually die, or disappear from the earth. As von der Vogelweide in "Vil Süze Wære Minne" writes: "Diu menscheit muoz verderben...got wolde dur uns sterben" (Wehrli 256) [Humanity must decay...God wanted for us to die]. Death is not only part of a natural cycle, but it is part of God's plan as well. Tolkien, being a devout Catholic, of course would have realised this. And in *The Lord of the Rings*, even the Elves, to whom the deities give immortality, must fade from the earth, or fade *into* it—blend slowly into its landscape. Entire races diminish in prelude to the rise of Men, who, in time, too will come to dwindle. Yet all of this does not result merely from the choices made by individuals: it is ordained by divine powers.

Many factors contribute to this process of dwindling, but one of the main catalysts to the process is this: when what once was (or appeared to be) "good" becomes or is found to be "evil," corruption and decay of the beholder and the world around him ensue. Walther von der Vogelweide dedicated an entire section of his elegy "Owê war sint verswunden alliu mîniu jâr" to this concept, lamenting:

> ...wie uns mit süezen   dingen ist vergeben!
> ich sihe die gallen mitten   in dem honege sweben:
> diu welt ist ûzen schœne,   wîz grüen unde rôt,
> und innan swarzer varwe,   vinster sam der tôt... (Wehrli 262)

[How we with sweet things become poisoned!/ I see gall swimming in the middle of the honey:/the world is outwardly beautiful: white, green, and red, / and inside of a black colour, darkness like unto death].

This should bring Tolkien's Silmarils to mind. The Silmarils "of their own radiance shone like the stars of Varda" (*The Silmarillion* 69) and encapsulate the mesmerising holy light of the Trees of Valinor. But soon Feanor begins to "love the Silmarils with a greedy love" (71) and poisons himself with their sweetness, withdrawing his kinship and honour as he withdraws the Silmarils from the sight of others, until finally, the objects which held potential for such great good become objects which instigate great evil.

It is not only external objects or creations that can become sour. The landscape itself is also an indication of corruption and evil: when the atmosphere is ominous, not only is the land itself evil but evil energy or evil beings are also nearby. As Tom Shippey writes: "Both characters and readers become aware of the extent and nature of Tolkien's moralisations from landscape"

(217). This makes perfect sense, because the earth itself is a living being, if not a conscious one. Tolkien hints at this by observing through his narrative such things as "living stone." In fact, when the world is created, it is given "a living heart of flame" (*Silmarillion* 9). So, where the earth is infected by the evil of Sauron—Mordor, for example—the landscape is sickly: rotted, smoky, and devoid of life.

This motif of something good having evil effects and manifesting through the environment is expanded upon in von der Vogelweide's poem addressed to "Frô Welt"—Lady World (Wehrli 252), of which there are several interpretations.

To summarise the poem, the (likely autobiographical) speaker "Walther" begins by addressing Frô Welt, telling her that he has become too obsessed with her and is tired of owing money to her landlord, whom he knows is keeping quiet until the day Walther will not be able to pay and then will come for him. The world, having through Walther's obsession taken on an actual personality and body (much like Tolkien's Ring is the physical manifestation of Sauron's will and the Silmarils are the physical manifestation of the creative energy of the Valar), tries to seduce him to stay, telling him he "zürnest âne nôt" (Wehrli 252) [is cross without need] and reminding him of all the wonderful things in life with which she provides him. However, Walther cannot be tricked, because he can see the evil beyond the beauty of Lady World, and reveals such understanding through the third stanza:

Frô Welt, ich hân ze vil gesogen:
ich wil entwonen, des ist zît.
dîn zart hât mich vil nâch betrogen,
wand er vil süezer fröiden gît.
do ich dich gesach reht under ougen,
dô was dîn schœne an ze schowen wünneclîch al sunder lougen:
doch was der schanden alse vil,
dô ich dîn hinden wart gewar, daz ich dich iemer schelten wil (Wehrli 252)

[Lady World, I have sucked too much:/I want to wean (myself), it is time (to do so)./Your tenderness has nearly deceived/betrayed me,/for it gives many sweet joys./As I saw directly in your face,/there was your beauty magnificent to look upon, undeniably,/but the shame was so much/ when I became aware of your back,/(that) I always want to curse you].

In this stanza, Walther reveals that he has discovered the world is, in fact, two-sided: beautiful and evil[2]. Thus caught, Lady World bids him farewell, asking only that he think of "manegen liehten tac" (Wehrli 252) [many a clear/bright day] and visit her when he is bored. Walther replies he would love to do so, but fears her spite or malice, from which no one can defend himself, then leaves for a "hereberge" (254)—a harbourage, likely Heaven (as he is leaving the world, so to speak)—and bids her farewell, saying "Gott geb Euch[3], Dame, gute Nacht" (254) [God give you, madam, good night].

As aforementioned, there are several interpretations of the poem as a whole. At their cores, they state basically either "Der Teufel hat ein Wirtshaus, genannt Welt; für die Freuden, die man darin genossen, muß man am Ende die Zeche bezahlen" (qtd. in Kartschoke 151) [the Devil has a hostelry named World; for the joys that one therein enjoys must one in the end pay the price] or "Die Welt ist eine Dirne, der Teufel ist ihr Zuhälter. Wer die Welt ,liebt'…, der steht bald beim Teufel" (151) [the world is a prostitute, the Devil is her pimp. Whosoever "loves" the world…(he) stands soon by the Devil]. The main difference, then, is that the world is either a trap set by the Devil himself, but does not take action directly (just as a house does not actively do anything), or the world is something actively working for the Devil. Perhaps, with Tolkien in mind, one could also interpret the poem as a not necessarily religious work: perhaps this "hereberge" is Faerie, and Walther wishes to leave the real world, to which he always owes pay—must follow its rules of society, physics, and reality. In any case, the story of Walther and Frô Welt is a test of will: when confronted with alluring, empowering evil in physical form, can a character maintain the reign of morality and goodness in his heart, and, if need be, leave the world altogether in order to preserve this morality? In Tolkien's *The Lord of the Rings,* Frodo eventually fails. But Walther manages to succeed, to prevail over temptation, much as figures such as Aragorn, Gandalf, and Galadriel do. Tolkien's story ends similarly to Walther von der Vogelweide's. Too much of the world is corruptive and evil: those who have been corrupted serve the Dark Lord Sauron; those who are good (the Elves and Frodo, for example) must eventually leave. Men are caught in between.

Another variant of this type of corruption through which good becomes evil is the corruption of power. Whether power itself corrupts or simply exposes is another argument which cannot be addressed here, but in any case, both J.R.R Tolkien and Walther von der Vogelweide write about characters wielding corrupt power. The greatest characters in *The Lord of the Rings* who are offered the Ring, Gandalf and Galadriel, already realize the evil powers thereof. When Frodo offers the Ring to Galadriel (who is without question good), she refuses, although she is tempted, because she understands what glory and malevolence she would be capable of: "I do not deny that my heart has greatly desired to ask what you offer," (*The Fellowship of the Ring* 356) she says, "and now…in place of the Dark Lord you will set up a Queen. And I shall not be dark, but beautiful and terrible as the Morning and the Night!…All shall love me and despair!" (356). And Gandalf responds similarly (though more sternly) when offered the Ring: "No!...With that power I should have power too great and terrible. And over me the Ring would gain a power still greater and more deadly....Do not tempt me!" (60).

While these characters resist the Ring altogether, the Ring's malevolently seductive powers are clear when the Fellowship takes up Boromir. Although Boromir initially has no evil intentions at heart (his greatest concern is Gondor), his temptation to take the Ring and become a great hero himself overcomes him. He tries to steal the Ring from Frodo and is killed soon after, scattering the members of the Fellowship and losing all hope of saving Gondor himself. The combination of the Ring and his own weakness—lust for power and greatness—are his downfall; he realizes this before his death, lying "still as if his own curse had struck him down; then suddenly he wept...'A madness took me, but it has passed'" (*Fellowship* 390).

The same corruption of power is seen in von der Vogelweide's work, conveyed succinctly in the following brief poem:

> Ahî wie kristenlîche nû der bâbest lachet
> swenne er sînen Walhen seit 'ich hânz alsô gemachet!'
> daz er dâ seit, des solt er niemer hân gedâht.
> er giht: 'ich hân zwên Almân under eine krône brâht,
> daz siz rîche sullen stœren unde wasten.
> ie dar under füllen wir die kasten:
> ich hâns an mînen stoc gement, ir guot ist allez mîn:
> ir tiuschez silber vert in mînen welschen schrîn.
> îr pfaffen, ezzent hüenr und trinkent wîn,
> unde lânt die tiutschen leien magern unde vasten!' (Wehrli 218-20)

[Ah, how Christianly the Pope now laughs,/whenever he says to his "Walhen"[4]: "I have made it so!"/Whatever he says there, he would have never thought it better./He says: "I have two Alemanni (tribes) under one crown brought,/so that they will destroy and wreak havoc upon the empire./Meanwhile we fill the bins:/I have pushed them to my offertory box; your good is all mine:/your German silver drives into my "welschen" (see footnote) shrine./You priests, eat chickens and drink wine/and let the German laity diminish and fast!].

In this poem, the Pope (whom von der Vogelweide often criticized) has abused his power and takes delight in it. He laughs "Christianly"—emphasizing the corruption of religion—and uses his power to bring civilizations to ruin and starve his people, while he and his priests feast. As the Pope is supposed to be in a position of benevolent power, this poem illustrates that even power with the greatest intentions can be corrupted.

Since the present is degraded by the progressive evil in the world, the past always seems to have been better. This leads to a powerful longing for the past and yearning to preserve the present so it cannot decay any further. It is important to note that both Faerie and the past are brought alive in the same manner—through the mind—so, it is impossible to distinguish for certain if one is longing for what actually happened in the Primary Reality, some event in Faerie that, in the reminiscer's mind, *seems* to have actually happened, or for an actual event flavoured and blended with the magic of Faerie. In any case, such longing for the past prevents one from fully living in the future and leads to great sadness. When comparing the current state of his people to their past, von der Vogelweide finds that those

den ê vil wünneclîchen   ir gemüete stuont!
die kunnen niuwan sorgen...
swar ich zer werlte kêre,   dâ ist nieman frô:
tanzen lachen singen   zergât mit sorgen gar (Wehrli 260-262)

[who once very high-hearted stood! –they know nothing but worries... whithersoever in the world I turn myself, there is no one joyful:/ dancing, laughing, singing pass by[5] all in worry].
This describes Tolkien's Elves quite well. While it is unclear how "high-hearted" they were to begin with—we are merely told that, when first introduced into the world, they "walked the Earth in wonder" (*Silmarillion* 45) and were "marvellous and unforeseen...stronger and greater than they have become" (46)—all of their activities, especially those that connect them to their past (such as singing), in *The Lord of the Rings* are laced with sorrow: practically every Elven song in *The Lord of the Rings* is melancholy or elegiac. And Elves everywhere—though some are more serious or unhappy than others—share the same underlying sorrow. The Numenoreans of Gondor also suffer this longing for the past, to the point that they "hungered after endless life unchanging" (*The Two Towers* 662) and "counted old names in the rolls of their descent dearer than the names of sons" (663). Excessive desire to return to the better days of the past fills the present with sorrow and takes the joy out of living—Walther von der Vogelweide and Tolkien both recognized this.

Although Primary Reality is doomed forever to degrade and bring sadness, there are ways to escape or transcend the decaying world. Religion (in Tolkien's case, Christianity) and the sea—though seemingly unrelated—are two paths commonly used by both Tolkien and von der Vogelweide that take one from Primary Reality into another realm.

Christianity, through death, takes one to Heaven. Whether or not this realm is connected to Faerie, no one living can truly say. Through life, Christianity connects one to God, and allows an individual to be helped and comforted by

Him. Understandably, Tolkien's fiction is thus brimming with cases of divine aid and intervention. The most obvious example is when Gandalf, a Maia, sacrifices himself to save the Fellowship from the Balrog. There are countless other cases, as divine forces are often dubbed "fortune" or "chance"—for example: "You have been saved, and all your friends too, mainly by good fortune" (*Towers* 579), Gandalf says to Pippen when he is released from the spell of the Palantir. Furthermore, deities can intervene by using mortals (or non-deities) to carry out their wills. As a case in point, Frodo is sent on his epic quest to fulfil the divine prophesies by helping to defeat evil in preparation for the Fourth Age. Walther von der Vogelweide also expresses this form of divine intervention in two lines: "got wil mit heldes handen/dort rechen sînen anden" (Wehrli 258) [God will with the hands of heroes avenge his blasphemy/dispraise]. Von der Vogelweide's other religious poems share the same basic themes with which Tolkien writes: God gives strength and passion ("uns mac dîn geist enzünden" (Wehrli 254) [us may Thy spirit ignite"]), God will help those in need ("got sol uns helfe erzeigen" (254) [God shall send us help]), and "bî swære ist gnâde funden" (256) [In need is mercy found]). Therefore, since God is all-powerful and can help anyone, despair is the ultimate sin—a form of *hubris*. Von der Vogelweide encourages man never to doubt God, as "swer sich von zwîvel kêret, der hât den geist bewart" (Wehrli 256) [who(soever) turns himself from doubt—he has kept/saved his spirit]. Such is the case with Frodo when he realizes the host of Morgul has departed to confront Faramir and his army (*Towers* 692). He is filled with despair and can do nothing but weep, until he beholds the holy light in the Phial of Galadriel and gains the strength to continue, despite the grim circumstances.

Religion is a vehicle that can deliver one from the corruption of the world, in life, and rescue one from the world itself, at death. The sea is vehicle of a similar type—it is commonly used to take one to the afterlife, or to Faerie. Perhaps it is because of this power that man is inherently drawn to the sea. Walther von der Vogelweide writes "wir gern zen swebenden ünden" (Wehrli 254) [We strive towards (or: "pursue") the surging sea].[6] Tolkien's characters are drawn to the sea as well, and "even his Wood-elf Legolas...acknowledges the powerful attraction of the sea....That same sea-longing haunts the Shire-bound Frodo...[and] the nameless voyager of Tolkien's early poem 'The Sea-bell'" (Flieger 163).

Of course, there are many possible reasons as to why people (and similar races) are so attracted to the sea, but one could safely assume that one of the main reasons is it leads to Faerie. After all, as creatures made in the image of a grand Creator, it is only natural that people (or Elves) would want to create as well. Therefore it is also natural that they should be enticed by any path to Faerie—the land where their creations become, in one sense or another, "real."

Indeed, there are examples of the sea taking one to Faerie (or possibly the afterlife, or Heaven) in both Tolkien's and von der Vogelweide's works.

An obvious example of the sea taking one into Faerie occurs in *The Return of the King*. Frodo, Gandalf, and several others, destined for the Undying Lands, sail "into the High Sea and pas[s] on into the West....And then it seemed to [Frodo] that as in his dream in the house of Bombadil...he beheld white shores and beyond them a far green country under a swift sunrise" (*The Return of the King* 1007). A journey across the sea takes Frodo and his company into a dream-like land, which precisely echoes Faerie. In a religious sense, this could also be the afterlife. Another example is found in *The Silmarillion*, when the hero Earendil (whose name means "lover of the sea" (*Silmarillion* 392)), finally sails to the land of the immortal with a Silmaril (297).

In each of these situations, a degree of sadness is present (likely related to Tolkien's use of the eucatastrophe—a bittersweet ending involving profound loss and a somewhat compensatory gain). This blend of emotions is captured most concisely at Frodo's departure when "amid his tears Pippin laughed" (*Return* 1007). And, of course, the transporting powers of the sea and the emotions at parting manifest at the end of von der Vogelweide's elegy "Owê war sint verswunden alliu mîniu jâr":

> sô wolte ich nôtic man   verdienen rîchen solt.
> joch meine ich niht die huoben   noch der hêrren golt:
> ich wolte sælden krône   êweclîchen tragen:
> …
> möht ich die lieben reise   gevaren über sê,
> sô wolte ich denne singen   wol und niemer mêr ouwê (Wehrli 264)

> [So shall I—a poor man—earn a rich pay./I certainly don't mean the courtyards or the gold of lords:/I shall (or: "want to." It somewhat unclear which is intended) the crown of blessedness eternally wear./.../ If I could make the dear journey over the sea,/then I would sing as such: "it is good!" and "nevermore, o woe!"].

Here, Von der Vogelweide connects the "dear journey" over the sea to eternally wearing the "crown of blessedness"—an obvious allusion to passing into the afterlife. The two phrases he chooses to sing, however, contradict each other completely, indicating the simultaneous joy and sadness of the situation.

Besides religion and the sea, time, memory, and dreams lie as bridges between Primary Reality and Faerie. Both reality and Faerie affect them, and can be reached through them. So, to understand these bridges and the second half of Figure 1 (above), Faerie and its nature must now be examined.

Faerie

Walther von der Vogelweide's elegy "Owê war sint verswunden alliu mîniu jâr," excerpted above and at the beginning of this study, paints a picture of the effects of Faerie in what one today could call a Tolkienian style. A main purpose of this Faerie is to pass on attributes such as wisdom to future generations. Walther von der Vogelweide laments, "Owê daz wîsheit unde jugent,/des mannes schœne noch sîn tugent/niht erben sol, sô ie der lîp erstirbet!" (Wehrli 206) [O woe, that (neither) wisdom nor youth,/the beauty of a human nor his ability/are inheritable, when each body dies away!], obviously wishing otherwise. Tolkien grants this wish. Throughout the cycles of Middle-Earth, people and objects are always reappearing—or their ancestors are inheriting their entire beings. The Silmarils become the rings. Sauron assumes the role of Melkor, and Saruman the former role of Sauron. Thingol and Melian reappear as Beren and Luthien, and, again, as Aragorn and Arwen. Moreover, this latter myth has its roots even deeper—in actual events from the creator's life: Tolkien made the love between himself and his wife eternal by making it a key myth in a mythic world (Birzer 23). A complete list of such "inheritances" in Tolkien's fiction would be all but endless. However, when these people and things reappear, they bring along their essential beauty, wisdom, skills, and powers. Verlyn Flieger refers to this phenomenon in the Elves as "serial longevity" (111). And it is through this "serial longevity" that conflicts and characters continue to live on and the Cauldron of Story continues to boil.

The Faerie of Tolkien and Walther von der Vogelweide share three key characteristics as well: first, it is impossible to discern for certain whether the events in Faerie "actually" happened; second, when one returns from Faerie, he cannot communicate his experience and the world seems hostile and uncaring; and third, there is great sorrow when one must leave Faerie, or discovers that it was a dream. "Ist mir mîn leben getroumet oder ist ez wâr?" (Wehrli 260) [Is my life dreamed or is it true?] asks Walther von der Vogelweide. This uncertainty haunts all who have been to Faerie—even when they are not aware they have made such a journey. Tolkien's Lothlorien and the land from which the adventurer in "The Sea-bell" returns produce the same effects as the vague realm to which von der Vogelweide refers: the visitor has dreamed, and yet he has not dreamed.

To understand this phenomenon, one must examine the origin of this realm. Whence does it come? A dream. But there is an interesting discrepancy as to *whose* dream. Max Wehrli translates the line quoted above as: "Habe ich mein Leben geträumt, oder ist es wahr?" (261). Translated into English, this is: "Have I dreamed my life, or is it true?" However, one must refer to the original text: von der Vogelweide, unlike Wehrli, uses a reflexive form of the verb *to dream*, and uses it in the passive voice. A translation of the original text ("Ist mir mîn leben getroumet oder ist ez wâr?") would be: "Is my life dreamed to me or is it true?"[7] Thus, it is unclear *who* has dreamed this life, if it is indeed a dream; so, although the reflexive verb form is often (even mostly) used with the subject and the indirect object being the same entity, Wehrli's assumption that the dream must come from the speaker in the poem (I would venture to say) is somewhat hasty.

This idea is expanded further in the following lines: "daz ich ie wânde daz iht wære, waz daz iht?/dar nâch hân ich geslâfen und enweiz es niht./nû bin ich erwachet…" (Wehrli 260) [What I always believed it were, was that (even) anything? So (or: "in such a way") have I slept and know nothing thereof. Now have I awakened]. What the speaker *believed* to be true, he now questions, wondering if it was indeed anything at all. *Anything at all*–as if all his beliefs were really just dreams? As if his beliefs had no substance—never actually happened at all? As if there was nothing real in the first place for him to believe? There are countless ways to interpret this idea. And he goes on to say that he slept but knew nothing thereof. If he was not aware that he even slept, he has no idea *how long* he has slept. Thus, he questions (quite rightly) if his entire life has been a dream. The parting scene between Gandalf and the hobbits in *The Return of the King* is reminiscent of this idea:

> 'Well here we are, just the four of us that started out together,' said Merry. 'We have left all the rest behind, one after another. It seems almost like a dream that has slowly faded.'
> 'Not to me,' said Frodo. 'To me it feels more like falling asleep again' (*Return* 974).

To Merry, the adventure seems as a dream; his life in the Shire is reality to him and he is finally returning to it. But to Frodo, the adventure is more real than the dreamland of the sheltered Shire: his quest completed, he now returns to the sleep-like state which has enveloped most of his life.

Because of its enigmatic and mirror-like nature, Faerie tangles Primary Reality and Secondary Reality together indistinguishably. Such is the case in Tokien's Lothlorien. Verlyn Flieger proposes that "Lorien itself is in a very real sense a dream sent or dreamed by the God of Dreams and that the Company in Lorien is, in one sense at least, inside that dream" (192). Again, one cannot say with certainty if this is the dream of Lorien, the Vala of dreams, or if it is a dream of the Elves, or the Company, only sent by Lorien. And just as in von der Vogelweide's elegy, one cannot be certain if the experience even *was* a dream. Sam, "rubbing his eyes as if he was not sure that he was awake" (*Fellowship* 342) says, "This is more elvish than anything I ever heard tell of. I feel as if I was *inside* a song, if you take my meaning" (342). Feeling as though he is inside a manifestation of dreams, myth, and/or magic—in this case, a "song"—he is just as puzzled as Walther von der Vogelweide as to the "reality" of his experience.

Further, one need not be in a designated Faerie-land: Eomer encounters the same strange feeling upon meeting Aragorn. "Dreams and legends spring to life out of the grass" (*Towers* 423), he says.

Several other properties of Faerie further blur distinction between Faerie and reality as well. Dreams, being connected with Faerie, allow "strange powers of the mind [to] be unlocked. In some of them a man may for a space wield the power of Faerie" ("On Fairy Stories" 116).

Since one travels often between dream and waking, one cannot for certain discern whether he has dreamed, or has not dreamed; whether he dreamed that he dreamed, or dreamed he had not; whether his entire reality is "real," or, in fact, Faerie—and so on. Furthermore stands the issue of time. In Tolkien's writings, time is "always 'happening' and [is] always in some sense 'present'" (Flieger 196). One could assume, then, that time is always "happening" in both the dream world and in Primary Reality. However, time seems to run at different rates. Walther von der Vogelweide (or the speaker in his elegy) awakens to find the land strange, forests destroyed, and his people unresponsive and old, yet he is unaware he has even slept for any amount of time. The adventurer in "The Sea-bell" returns to similar conditions; "he is estranged from his own world" (Flieger 208) and "suddenly old" (207), forced to wander about in wretchedness.

The relation between Primary Reality and Faerie is further complicated by the fact that each can affect the other. For example, while resting in the marshes, Frodo awakens and "fe[els] refreshed. He had been dreaming. The dark shadow had passed, and a fair vision had visited him in this land of disease. Nothing remained of it in his memory, yet because of it he felt glad and lighter of heart" (*Towers* 620). In von der Vogelweide's elegy, details of his dream (if it is in fact a dream) are not given either, but he longs to return to it, and grieves its disappearance: "als ich gedenke an manegen wünneclîchen tac,/die mir sint enphallen…/iemer mêr ouwê" (Wehrli 260) [So I think of many a joy-filled day/that has slipped from me…/forever(more), o woe!]. Of course, the details of the dream must not always be so obscure to affect reality—in *The Fellowship of the Ring*, for example, Merry awakens after a rather graphic dream of being a warrior from earlier times, stabbed in the chest with a spear, and still believes he is wounded for several seconds. In fact, he retains the entire reality of the warrior for these moments, recalling in an archaic tongue how his host was "worsted." Obviously the confusion between dream and reality when Faerie is involved has rather complex causes—far too complex to be covered in any degree of thoroughness in this study. However, the other two effects of Faerie mentioned earlier must not be forgotten: Faerie is incommunicable, and it brings great sadness and disillusionment upon departure.

Tolkien's fiction manifests the inexplicability of Faerie through several characters: Sam, who struggles but cannot describe Lothlorien exactly; Pippen, who, although not exactly in "Faerie" *per se*, cannot put into words the Faerie-like effects Treebeard's eyes have on him; and the wanderer in "The Sea-bell," who is forced to drift about, talking to himself, because no one can possibly understand. This effect is crafted more subtly in Walther von der Vogelweide's elegy, when he states, "mich grüezet maneger trâge, der mich bekande ê wol./diu welt ist allenthalben ungenâden vol" (Wehrli 260) [Dully[8] some greet me, some who once knew me well./The world is everywhere full of ill will[9]]. Former friends now greet the speaker disinterestedly—one could assume they do not understand, or simply no longer care about him. Moreover, the world seems full of ill will (see footnote) or general hostility, alienating the speaker further. Finally, when one must leave Faerie or when one discovers the so-called "dark side" of Faerie (Flieger 217-19), there is a great sense of sorrow. Examples of this in Tolkien's writings occur when the adventurer of "The Sea-bell" is exploring Faerie, and "the ambient beauty darkens....Passing in a moment from joyous summer to bleak winter, he passes also from eager youth to disappointed age" (Flieger 207-8), and in *The Lord of the Rings*, when the Fellowship leaves Lorien with "their eyes...dazzled, for all were filled with tears" (*Fellowship* 369). Walther von der Vogelweide's elegy ends in the same sorrow. After finding the world changed—full of sorrow and hostility—and understanding that what he once thought to be sweet now poisons, he yearns to sail over the sea, singing, "it is good!" and "nevermore, o woe!" (Wehrli 264). This latter phrase of sadness he then repeats, closing the elegy and leaving the reader in sentimental sorrow, probably the same kind of feeling both his speaker and Tolkien's characters are left with after their experiences.

Thus, one leaves Faerie, but Faerie itself never truly comes to an end, as it continues through time, at whatever rate. Faerie lives on through memory and dreams, often—like history—becoming myth and therefore indistinguishable from "real" past events and "Faerie" events. For, truly, Faerie *must* be given up, or exited, to be passed on as it is. Walther von der Vogelweide had to awaken before he could recall the strangeness of the dream he (possibly) experienced. The Fellowship must leave Lothlorien in order to use the knowledge they gain inside the beautifully strange land. And Tolkien himself had to leave Faerie—that is, end the tale of *The Lord of the Rings* and publish it—to pass it on to his readers worldwide.

Faerie is everywhere, both in stories and "real life." Whenever one—no matter how briefly, no matter if only "in his head"—experiences something outside the immediate physical world, he has experienced Faerie, and sometimes, he can become completely enchanted and fully enter the realm where sub-creations of an imagination become real in one sense or another.

Tolkien wrote about the Cauldron of Story, in which elements of Faerie from all times and places brew. Walther von der Vogelweide's elements boiled for hundreds of years before Tolkien served them up in his amazing myths. Or, perhaps, Tolkien and von der Vogelweide both partook of the same stew, a rich potage as ancient as the Cauldron itself.

MONTANA STATE UNIVERSITY

WORKS CONSULTED

Birzer, Bradley J. *J.R.R Tolkien's Sanctifying Myth: Understanding Middle-Earth.* Wilmington: ISI Books, 2003.

Das Digitale Wörterbuch der deutschen Sprache des 20. Jahrhunderts. Hans Magnus Enzensberger et al., eds. Nov. 2004. Berlin-Brandenburgische Akadamie der Wissenschaften. 26 Mar. 2005. <http://www.dwds.de>.

Flieger, Verlyn. *A Question of Time: J.R.R. Tolkien's Road to Faerie.* Kent: Kent State UP, 1997.

Kartschoke, Dieter. "*gedenke an mangen liebten tac:* Walthers Abschied von Frau Welt L 100, 24 ff." *Walther Lesen: Interpretationen und Überlegungen zu Walther von der Vogelweide.* Volker Mertens and Ulrich Müller, eds. Göppingen: Kümmerle Verlag, 2001. Pp. 147-66.

Koepke, Wulf. *Die Deutschen: Vergangenheit und Gegenwart.* 5th ed. Boston: Thomson-Heinle, 2000.

Lexer, Matthias. *Mittelhochdeutsches Handwörterbuch.* 2002. Deutsche Forschungsgemeinschaft, Universität Trier. 25 Apr. 2005. <http://germazope.uni-trier.de/Projects/WBB/woerterbuecher/lexer/wbgui?lemid=LA00001>.

Shippey, Tom. *The Road to Middle-Earth: How J.R.R. Tolkien created a new mythology.* Rev. and exp. ed. New York: Houghton Mifflin, 2003.

Tolkien, J.R.R. *The Fellowship of the Ring.* New York: Houghton Mifflin, 1994.

_____. "On Fairy Stories." *The Monsters and the Critics.* Ed. Christopher Tolkien. London: HarperCollins, 1997. Pp. 109-62.

_____. *The Return of the King.* New York: Houghton Mifflin, 1994.

_____. *The Silmarillion.* Ed. Christopher Tolkien. New York: Ballantine, 1999.

_____. *The Two Towers.* New York: Houghton Mifflin, 1994.

Wehrli, Max, ed. *Deutsche Lyrik des Mittelalters.* Zürich: Manesse Verlag, 1962.

NOTES

[1] Tolkien defines Faerie as "the realm or state in which fairies have their being...it holds...the earth, and all things that are in it...and ourselves, mortal men, when we are enchanted" ("On Fairy Stories" 113). He adds, "An essential power of Faerie is thus the power of making immediately effective by the will the visions of 'fantasy'" (122)—which,

in essence, means that it is the realm in which an invented Secondary Reality exists, or is "immediately effective."

[2] Though such an image appears in many places throughout literature, Dietrich Kartschoke, referring to the work of G. Thiel, writes that the image of Lady World, "deren Anblick von vorn so erfreulich wie von hinten scheußlich ist, erscheint hier zum ersten Mal in der Literatur" (150) [whose appearance from in front is as joyous as from in back (it is) horrid/nasty/rotten, appears here for the first time in literature]. Perhaps von der Vogelweide himself created or discovered this image in his own world of Faerie.

[3] *Euch (iu* in the original, a variant of *iuch*) (Lexer) is the plural informal accusative (direct object) or dative (indirect object) word for *you*. Walther could be referring to the world and everything she includes, therefore using the plural, or referring to her in the plural as royalty, as the formal or polite form of *you, Sie*, did not come into use until several centuries later (Koepke). Furthermore, as the objective case of *euch* is not clear, whether Walther is wishing God gives *to* Lady World or gives Lady World herself is also open to interpretation.

[4] I have not been able to find anything on the word *Walhen*, or on Wehrli's interpretation: *Welschen*. In any case, it seems to be a group of people he is addressing, possibly his followers.

[5] It is interesting that Wehrli translates the word *zergât* into modern German as *vergeht*, which means most commonly to pass/go by or elapse, though it can also mean to wear down/away, etc.. The modern word *zergeht (zergehen)*, a direct derivative of *zergât*, means to dwindle, or to melt away. The difference between these interpretations is that the events are either simply taking place in sorrow, for which Wehrli's translation allows, or fading in sorrow from occurrence altogether, which is more strongly indicated in the original text, yet still viable through Wehrli's translation as well.

[6] Wehrli translates this line as "wir streben zum wogenden Meer" (255), which is what I have translated to English here. However, the meaning of the original text may be slightly different. Von der Vogelweide does not mention the sea directly; he refers to it (as is common German practice) as the adjective *swebenden* (from the verb *sweben*), which Wehrli has interpreted as *wogenden*. While I am unaware of the exact meaning of *sweben*, it may be worth mentioning that it is similar to other appropriate German words: *weben*, to weave (as the initial *s* from many words beginning with *sw* was dropped over time); *schweben*, to waver; *schwimmen*, to swim (as Wehrli translates it elsewhere; see page 3).

Furthermore, the word *gern* implies that the verb is done gladly. Matthias Lexer translates the verb *ünden* as "*fluten, wogen, wellen schlagen."* (*to flood, to surge/wave, waves crashing*). Therefore, "wir gern zen swebenden ünden" can be translated as "we eagerly/gladly flood to the surging (sea)." This is interesting, because it implies that the people are just as fluid as the waves themselves, yielding a sense of unity between the earth and its inhabitants, life and what lies beyond it.

[7] It is also interesting to note that, in both cases, the verb *dream* is in the present perfect tense, while *be* is used in the simple present tense. Thus, although the act of dreaming is something already experienced, the dream itself (or the life) is something still present, still happening.

8 Wehrli uses the word *säumig*, which translates roughly to *belatedly*. However, the original text uses *trâge*, the root of modern German *träge*: *dully, languidly, lazily,* etc.

9 Wehrli translates *ungenâden* as *Mißgunst*: malevolence, ill will, or even jealousy or distrust. *Ungenâden*, however, is the root of the modern *Ungnade* (from *genâden*, *Gnade: graciousness*), which would mean *ungraciousness*, a seemingly less harsh word than in Wehrli's translation; however, it is possible the strength of the word changed over time.

From Waste Land to Grail and Back Again:
Naomi Mitchison's *To The Chapel Perilous*

Peter G. Christensen

What is the Holy Grail and what are its origins? We are used to having scholars discuss these questions but less accustomed to having a novelist do so. However, this is the case with *To the Chapel Perilous* (1955) by Naomi Mitchison (1897-1999), a modern novel about the Holy Grail republished by Green Knight Press in recent years.[1] The reprinting has already prompted two essays on Mitchison's novel, one by Michael D. Amey in *Arthuriana* and one by Anita Overmeier forthcoming in *Studies in Medievalism*. *To the Chapel Perilous* was reviewed with other reprinted Arthturian novels in the Winter 2001 issue of *Arthuriana* by Alan Lupack, who found that, through Mitchison's contention that "both the Church and economic forces have a vested interest in having One Grail Knight, one version of the story," the novel offers "postmodern skepticism about the reliability of a received story" and "foreshadow[s] later works like Barthelme's *The King*" (140).

I would like to present here another way of looking at *To the Chapel Perilous*, one which stresses the novel's modernism. Mitchison is not just concerned here with skepticism about a real story. In advocating a view that each person must be committed to his/her own view of the Grail, Mitchsion is also making a case that the ritual-school view of the Grail derived from Jessie Weston and from the Cambridge school of early 20[th-]century anthropology is superior to the traditional Christian view. To do so, Mitchison extends the waste land motif, a relatively small aspect of the motif of the religious quest around the Grail that she takes from Malory's *Morte Darthur*. Second, she makes the pagan Grails more impressive than the Christian. Third, she specifically uses the work of Jessie L. Weston and Robert Graves, as she admits in interview material.

For background, a brief discussion of the criticism of Raymond H. Thompson and Marilyn K. Nellis on *To the Chapel Perilous* is in order. Thompson has done more than anyone to call deserved attention to Mitchison's novel. Back in 1985, he examined it in his chapter on "Fantasy" in *The Return from Avalon: A Study of the Arthurian Legend in Modern Fiction*.[2] He also wrote the Introduction to the 1999 reprint, interviewed Lady Mitchison in 1999 (she died later that year) for his collection of Camelot Project interviews, and discussed the novel in his essay, "The Grail in Modern Fiction: Sacred Symbol in a Secular Age," which appeared in *The Grail: A Casebook* (2000), edited by Dhira B. Mahoney. In his 1985 work, Thompson claimed that a major theme of the novel was that the Grail legend must be rediscovered by each individual. As he notes in his later article, "conflicting stories and political manipulation" (2000: 555) led to the establishment of the Church's version of the Grail story as the accepted one. As they send back stories, the newspaper reporters have to keep in mind powerful institutions (such as the Church) and individuals, advertisers, readers, editors, and subeditors (556).[3]

Michel D. Amey, in his 2004 *Arthuriana* article on Mitchison's novel, stresses the liberating power of the text. He believes that Mitchison "exposes the interdependent relationship between knowledge and power and the manner in which they construct dominant discourses of reality and truth" (69). For him, the author "provides the blueprint for building a truly perilous chapel in which truth and reality are revealed to be contingent on the lived experiences of individuals" (69). My viewpoint is very different, for I claim that, instead of actually calling upon the individualized "lived experiences" of people with their different ideas of the nature of the Grail suitable to their specific circumstances, Mitchison relies on the pre-existing formulations of the Frazerian school of anthropology, now shown to be methodologically inept, for her major examples.

In her interview with Thompson, Mitchison asserts her preference for Malory's version of Arthurian materials over Tennyson's. She mentions that she knew Robert Graves personally, corresponded with him, and based her figure of the White Lady in the novel in part on his figure of the White Goddess. She also states that she was a reader of Jessie L. Weston's *From Ritual to Romance*, but that she did not make any intensive study of the Grail legends in order to write her novel. She was already familiar with Irish and Welsh materials upon which she could draw to write the novel, which she composed very rapidly during a trip to the United States. A promoter of respect and tolerance, she was suspicious of organized religion and of the power of the Christian Church. Her concern with tolerance is discussed by the one other critic who analyzes the novel in detail, Marilyn K. Nellis, in "Anachronistic Humor in Two Arthurian Romances of Education: *To the Chapel Perilous* and *The Sword in the Stone*" (1983). She writes:

> If only commitment locates a truth [,] and objectivity cannot be put into action in the world because of intolerance, [then] detachment must be rejected as a model of personal development, [and] thought commitment should never be pursued to the point of interfering with another person's development (61).

Nellis, as well as Thompson and Lupack, relies on accepting the views of the protagonists, Lienors and Dalyn, at the end of the story when they discuss the waste land as the key to the novel's message.

The Waste Land as such is not mentioned much by Malory. It appears first in the story of Balin, the Knight with Two Swords, where it is associated wth the Dolorous Stroke, and later during the quest for the Holy Grail. In the first instance, we read:

> So whan Balyn saw the spere he gate hit in hys honde and turned to
> kynge Pellam and felde hym and smote hym passyngly sore with that
> spere, that kynge Pellam [felle] downe in a sowghe. And therewith the
> castell brake rooffe and wallis and felle downe to the erthe. And Balyn
> felle downe and might nat styrre hande nor foote, and for the moste
> party of that castell was dede thorow the dolorouse stroke. (Malory
> 1971: Book 2, p. 53 lines 38-43)

In the next paragraphs we hear more about the Dolorous Stroke, Longinus,
Christ, and Joseph of Arimathea. When King Pellam, a kinsman of Joseph, is
injured, the region nearby suffers. Malory writes, "and grete pité hit was of
hys hurte, for thorow that stroke hit turned to grete dole, tray and tene" (54.
12-13).

> When we hear of the Dolorous Stroke again, it is specifically related
> to the "Waste Londe." Sir Percival's sister gives this description of it
> to her brother: 'And hit was in the realme of Logris, and so befelle
> there grete pestilence, and grete harme to bothe reallmys; for there
> encresed nother corne, ne grasse, nother well-nye no fruyte, ne in the
> watir was founde no fyssh. Therefore men calle hit—the londys of
> the two marchys—the Waste Londe, for that dolorous stroke. (Book
> 18; 581.31)

Malory has Galahad, not Percival, describe the origin of the sword, an origin
not found in the French *Queste* (Ihle 137). As D. Thomas Hanks points out, it
is significant that the sword travels from Balin to Galahad (97). When Galahad
heals the Maimed King and restores the Waste Land, as Muriel Whitaker says,
it is an event which "combines Christian allegory with Celtic myth" (72) (Book
17; 604.15). In Malory's context, the end of the Grail quest has naturally a much
greater Christian emphasis than a Celtic pagan one. Mitchison, on the other
hand, emphasizes the Celtic strain in her novel, and we need to look beyond
the words of Mitchison's protagonists to completely understand her view of
the Grail and to see how she deemphasizes the Christian view of it.

First, Mitchison both introduces and concludes her novel with a secular
waste land motif, thus reducing the importance of the religious quest for the
Grail carried over from Malory. The novel's protagonists are two newspaper
reporters, Lienors Blanchmains, who works for Merlin's *Camelot Chronicle,* and
Dalyn, who is employed by the rival newspaper, the *Northern Pict*, edited by
Lord Horny, the Devil. The *Camelot Chronicle* has good connections with the
Court and the Church, whereas the *Northern Pict* does not. Lienors and Dalyn,
who are romantically attracted to each other, have been on assignment in a
waste land near the Chapel Perilous for many months, out of contact with almost
everyone except a mysterious hermit. Suddenly, the waste land disappears as
not just one but five Grail knights leave the Castle Perilous with their own
particular Grail. In addition to Galahad, Gawain, Lancelot, Perceval, and Bors

all get a Grail, which they take back home with them. However, the Grail as object varies from person to person. It has as incarnations Gawain's cauldron of plenty; Lancelot's cup and spear, which heal people (suggesting fertility symbols as well as items related to Christ's Passion); Perceval/Peredur's shining stone, which spills gold; Bors's Dish of the Last Supper; and Galahad's mysterious, covered object which frees the souls of the dead at Halloween mass.

In the first half of the novel, action is injected into what could potentially be rather static scenes of visits to Gawain's Spiral Castle, Lancelot's Joyous Garde, Perceval/Peredur's Forêt Sauvage, Bors's Castle Bran de Gore, and Galahad's Corbyn, all through Lienors's involvement with Camelot's politics. She prefers Gawain to Mordred when it comes to Arthur's possible heirs. She sympathizes with the adulterous Lancelot and Guinevere, even though she has been responsible through her reportage of making Galahad's, not Lancelot's, Grail the one and only real Grail. Her articles inevitably set her against Elayne of Corbyn, who, married to Lancelot, despises Guinevere. Although Lienors takes Guinevere in secret to see Lancelot's presentation of his Grail to the public, the Queen mistakenly later thinks that Lienors has betrayed her trust, after Lienors tells Lancelot of Guinevere's trip to see his Grail.

As Lancelot heads to Camelot at Christmas, near Oxford he meets up with the Brothers from Orkney. It seems from their brief conversation that news of Guinevere's appearance at Joyous Guard to see Lancelot's Grail has leaked out and annoyed Morgan-Morgause, who has never liked Guinevere and who fears that such news will detract from her son Gawain's Cauldron of Ceridwen (130). Guinevere can potentially interfere in the case of Gawain or one of his brothers becoming heir to Arthur's realm. (The novel does not present Mordred as Arthur's son through incest with his sister but rather as his nephew.) Later, Morgan-Morgause, after the discovery of Lancelot in Guinevere's room, councils Arthur to have Guinevere burned at the stake. The narrator gives this material indirectly:

> The King had gone into a small locked room by himself to think it out, away from the voices, and in the room was his sister Queen Morgan-Morgause[,] and her sons knew nothing of it. She took her brother Arthur into her arms and the old pattern that was before kings and queens, before Saxons and Romans, before the standing stones, the old pattern repeated itself. Guinevere was no part of this pattern of succession; she never had been. (148)

Arthur chooses Morgan-Morgause's advice over that of his best knights, a situation that has no parallel in Malory. Thus, the Great Mother acts to help bring down Camelot.

It is never explained what is meant here by the word "pattern," although it seems to be associated with the rule of the Great Mother. Nevertheless, the use of the word "pattern" is noteworthy here since it recurs in Lienors's big speech to Dalyn on the way to Amesbury:

> But you see, Dalyn, all these—various sources of ours, including
> the respectable ones—are different patterns that people can
> make themselves into. Or be made into if they aren't strong and
> knowledgeable. And each pattern uncovers a different aspect of the
> heart: a different means of wisdom. . . .And each pattern is dangerous
> to the other patterns and must seem hateful to their followers. Unless
> to the very wise and tolerant people. (202)

Here the "pattern" suggests and justifies views other than the official Catholic
hierarchy's view of Galahad's 'one true Grail.' Lienors continues, saying that
most people are too frightened to be tolerant, and so at any given time there
is always one pattern that dominates (202). She mentions St. Columba as a
possible example of a tolerant person, a comment which is significant as he was
mentioned once earlier in the novel. Lady Julia, wife of Sir Bors, had unfairly
disparaged St. Columba for not knowing that "Rome is always right" and for
mixing ideas "older than the Church" with Roman Catholicism (95).

In the second half of the novel, before we get back to the waste land, the
pace speeds up remarkably, as we learn of key events recorded by Malory, such
as the discovery of Lancelot without his armor in Guinevere's room, followed
by the death of Agravaine in Lancelot's escape. Malory's general plot outline
is followed as Gawain becomes a fierce enemy of Lancelot, and Gaheris and
Gareth are killed in the fighting when Guinevere is rescued by Lancelot from
being burned at the stake. Mordred declares himself ruler while Arthur is in
France, forcing Guinevere, who refuses to marry him, to retreat to the Tower
to resist him. Arthur kills Mordred on Salisbury Plain in the last battle, and,
severely wounded himself, he then calls upon Bedivere to throw his sword
into the water.

Dalyn is wounded on Salisbury Plain and sees Arthur's sword taken by the
Lady of the Lake, as well as Arthur's departure in the barge with the Weeping
Women. In addition, an important detail is added which functions as a corrective
to Malory's version. On the barge, four women with Morgan-Morgause hold
up in their arms "the Grail, the Cauldron of Ceridwen, the cauldron perhaps
of healing and perpetual youth" (191).

As we see in the second half of the novel, the Grail appearances have
helped to speed up the fall of Camelot. We have only one pointed statement
about it. After being wounded, Dalyn says, "Everything had been going
splendidly...till the Grail story" (191). Dalyn thinks, "And this Grail [is] breaking
up everything that seemed durable and splendid, the Round Table, the life of
Camelot" (191). However, Mitchison does not explain why Dalyn thinks that
the Grail has been so destructive. When we look at the Grail knights late in
the novel, as in Malory's last tale, the main opposition is between Lancelot
and Gawain. In each case, Perceval and Galahad are gone, and Bors takes
Lancelot's side and outlives both him and Gawain.

Meanwhile, Lienors, who had been kidnapped by agents of the Archbishop, was not free to get involved in the final events of Camelot until Merlin promised to accept for his newspaper the Catholic Church's version of Galahad's vision of the Grail in Sarras and his translation to heaven. Lienors hunts for Dalyn on the battlefield, finds him, and helps Queen Guinevere sew up his wound.

Dalyn and Lienors witness the last meeting of Lancelot and Guinevere after Guinevere has retired to the convent at Amesbury. Finally, Dalyn and Lienors set out to find Arthur's grave in Avalon, but they do not find it and arrive again where they started, at a waste land by the Chapel Perilous. They receive words of wisdom from the hermit, who assures them that the Church's presentation of the events at Sarras was a staged hoax. The conversation between the three characters as the waste land starts to bloom again, as well as the earlier conversation between Dalyn and Lienors on their way to Amesbury, has been considered by Thompson and Nellis to summarize the theme of the novel, that is, of the importance of personal involvement in individualized Grail quests, maintained in a spirit of tolerance.

In the last chapter, Dalyn's view that the Grail broke up everything seems to be gainsaid, at first glance, by the long speech of the hermit, who goes even farther than St. Columba once did in offering a tolerant Catholicism:

> It [The wasteland] blossoms, as you know, with the ending of the quest, the finding of the Grail. And that palpably so that it can be reported and has been. Equally, the wound is healed, the secret told, the riddle becomes plain, the reconciliation is made between man and what surrounds him. Each happening depends on the other. But if it was for all time, the flowers might go on blooming but the spirit would wither. It would be sad beyond all telling if the finding of the Grail were to happen once for all. Because then it could not happen again for anyone. (217)

However, we should remember that the hermit is not interested in the fall of Camelot, which is a Christian community which flourishes once and dies. He is only concerned with the eternal pattern of waste land and fertile land, so the novel can end with the line, "Yes, thought the hermit, the quest seems to be going well" as flowers bloom and birds court (219).

Second, to diminish the Christian view of the Grail, between the flowerings of the waste land, Mitchison makes the pagan Grails more impressive than the Christian. Mitchison arranges the five Grails in order from least Christian or most pagan to most Christian, while at the same time showing that the pagan Grails bring more joy. Mitchison retains from Malory five Grail knights of primary importance, Gawain, Lancelot, Perceval, Bors, and Galahad. Lienors and Dalyn visit them in that order. In Malory, Gawain is the least successful on the Grail quest. Lancelot, because of his love for Queen Guinevere, is less successful than Bors and Percival. Galahad is the greatest hero of the Quest.

Mitchison, however, follows an order of presentation that undercuts Malory's hierarchy of winners and losers. The Winchester manuscript concentrates on Perceval, Lancelot, Gawain, Bors, and Galahad in that order before taking the story to the Castle of Corbenic and then to Sarras for the miracle of Galahad. This arrangement is quite different than Mitchison's, for she prefers Gawain and Lancelot to the other three, who are more successful in Malory's version. Her order moves basically upward from the bottom of Malory's hierarchy from losers to winners, placing Perceval before Bors in the middle.

The more joyous scenes are associated with Gawain and Lancelot rather than with Perceval, Bors, and Galahad. Gawain's Cauldron is specifically designated at the Cauldron of Plenty (1999: 38, 39), which once belonged to Ceridwen. (See "The Tale of Taliessin" translated by Patrick K. Ford [1979] for Ceridwen's Cauldron.) This Grail is associated with Gawain because he is from Celtic Scotland and because his mother is a combination Morgan-Morgause figure (44-45), which is not so in Malory's romance.

At Gawain's Spiral Castle, the celebration is mostly joyful, but not completely so. There is much singing, dancing, eating, and music making. However, no one can control the gifts, and some people receive improbable or unpleasant presents. Whereas Gareth gets an elephant's trunk, Gawain has a beautiful branch of snow flakes. Some people receive useful gifts, but others end up with a dragon's egg or a small green half-man. At the end, Gawain becomes tired. His mother tries to get him to take a virgin, but he declines. People then fall asleep or go home. The scene provides a take-off on Launcelot's first appearance at Corbyn when the holy vessel provides "all manner of meates and drynkes that they coude thynke upon" (Malory 479 [Caxton 11.1])

At Joyous Garde, Lancelot, empowered with the gift of healing by the Grail, offers the most emotionally moving ceremony of the five Grail Knights. After he plunges a spear into a deep silver cup seven times, the spear begins to drip with blood, and it is placed in a white cloth (64-65). Then, the sick are carried to Lancelot and healed, "partly or wholly" (660) including a young man who had been attacked by a wolf. Except for Elayne, who screams as Lancelot makes the third stroke with the spear, everyone seems impressed. Eventually the healing force is drained from Lancelot's body and he stops. Lancelot does more immediate good than any of the other Grail knights. (Perhaps Malory's episode of Lancelot healing of Sir Urrey was in Mitchison's mind here.) He has the objects associated with both fertility rituals and Christ's Passion. However, because of Elayne's scream, the sexual symbols seem more important.

The Grails of Malory's three more successful knights have a less pleasing effect. At the Forêt Sauvage Peredur goes down into a cave-tomb with two companions. Peredur kills a snake, while his companions slay opponents in "curious armour of overlapping scales, something oddly out of date" (84). In *Le Morte Darthur* on the Grail Quest, Percivale dreamt of a serpent and a lion (Malory 546 [Caxton 14.6]). Kundrie, the Flower Maiden, goes through contortions in the background. When Peredur and Kundrie hold up a Grail which is a shining stone on a heap of gold, the crowd starts rushing through, scrambling for the gold. When the people depart, there is no sign of where the dead bodies and dead dragon have gone (85). The reader suspects some deceit.

Next, there seems to be no useful effect when Sir Bors offers Communion from his Grail at Castle Bran de Gore. (According to Welsh myth, Bran ruled eastern Britain, and, once a Celtic god, he became a prototype of the Fisher King). Gore, here, seems to have nothing to do with Urien's northern realm of Gore in the *Morte Darthur*. The rite is performed in a hot, stuffy chapel, and the Grail is a "flat dish, silver, very plain and old and a little battered" (100). A priest kneels and prays on one side, while King Bran, Bors's father, does so on the other. Communion does not make a big spiritual impression, since the effects of the Eucharist are not described (100). Soon after, there is a harvest time vigil, at which the Old King dies, touching the Grail. However, at the same time Bors's son, Helian le Blanc (Elyne le Blanke in Malory 504 [Caxton 12.9]), is tormented by desires of the flesh, associated with the fertility of the field.

Finally, Galahad's Grail at Corbyn[4] is used in both a Halloween All Souls' mass and at mass the next day, All Saints'. At the Halloween mass, the ghosts of the past are raised in what Lienors calls a harrowing of Hell (123). Before the masses, King Pelles, the Fisher King, had been cured by the Grail. (In Le Morte Darthur Galahad cured the Maimed Knight with blood from the spear, cf. Malory 604 [Caxton 17.20]).When Elayne, Galahad's mother, sees Lienors, she breaks into a fury, which reflects her secret fear that Lancelot's healing Grail is more impressive than her son's. Indeed, readers will probably feel that she is right. The healing of the Fisher King has only limited effect, as it has no connection at this ceremony to the revival of a waste land. Again, as in the case with Bors, Holy Communion does not seem to have any strong effect on anyone.

Mitchison allows the Cauldron of Ceridwen and the fertility symbols of the ritual approach to the Grail to offer at least as much, and in Lancelot's case more, to the people than the ceremonies of Bors and Galahad, which involve church masses. The stone at the Forêt Sauvage, is taken, like Kundrie, from Wolfram von Eschenbach's *Parzifal*, where the Grail is a stone. As in the case of Parzifal's stone, which has associations outside of the novel with the angels who chose not to take sides in the struggle between God and Satan, Mitchison works with Grail objects that have already come down from myth and legend. She does not make up any new ones, although Dalyn and Lienors suggest that each person should have his own particular Grail.

Third, as Mitchison admitted in her interview with Thompson, she was influenced by Jessie L. Weston and Robert Graves, and her non-Christian Grails, which de-emphasize Christianity, reflect these sources. Weston devotes all of her Chapter 13 of *From Ritual to Romance* to "The Perilous Chapel," and Mitchison uses one of the key ideas from it. For Weston, "the Mystery ritual comprised a double initiation, the Lower, into the mysteries of generation, *i. e.* of physical Life; the higher, into Spiritual Divine Life, where man is made one with God." The Perilous Chapel, for Weston, represents the site of the first, lower, or physical initiation, and it involves a "[c]ontact with the horrors of physical death" (182). In the novel's first chapter, the Chapel Perilous is described as "the most spectacular of the dangers," a place where there has been "death and madness" (14). Here, ladies threw themselves in grief over knights who have been killed, and the young and handsome came out ravaged. Although she felt that the treasures of the Celtic Tuatha de Danaan corresponded with the four Grail symbols (cup, lance, sword, and dish), Weston did not want to equate the Cauldron with the Grail (77), for she found "no direct connection between these Celtic objects and the Grail story" (77). Mitchison makes that imaginative leap in making the Cauldron one of the five forms of the Grail in her novel.

The setting of Mitchison's second chapter, "The Spiral Castle" seems inspired less by Weston than by Robert Graves's chapter, "A Visit to Spiral Castle" in *The White Goddess*. Both Graves and Weston were heavily indebted to the work of Sir James Frazer, whom they each cite several times. Mitchison had already relied on Frazer and the Cambridge anthropologists in her novel *The Corn King and the Spring Queen*. Graves, in his typical imaginative manner, connects the fortress at New Grange in Brugh-na-Boyne, Ireland, to the White Goddess by the intermediary step of relating the Irish Sidhe to the Welsh Caer Sidi, or Revolving Castle (97). Later in the same chapter, he associates these castles with the White Goddess, incarnated as Morgan le Faye, and thus with her isle of Avalon, where she takes King Arthur (105). The same chapter discusses the poem, supposedly by Taliesin (this bard is also mentioned in the novel), "Preiddeu Annwn" ("The Spoils of Annwn"). This poem mentions Prydwen, which Graves calls the magic ship or barge which takes Arthur to Avalon. Although in *To the Chapel Perilous* the castle of Gawain and his mother Morgan-Morgause is in Scotland, as a Celtic country, Scotland replaces the Ireland and Wales discussed by Graves.

There are only brief references to the White Lady, Graves's White Goddess, in the course of *To the Chapel Perilous* (17, 45, 56, 88, 202). Some of these are mysterious. For example, Dalyn asks Lienors outside the Chapel Perilous if there is any news from Camelot.

"You know, the White Lady---" said Lienors, and hesitated.

"What's She done now?" Dalyn asked.

"I saw the mark. With my own eyes," said Lienors. "Someone you'd never expect. It was Her all right."

"You can't put that in, dear," said Dalyn, "not about the White Lady. Besides it ``isn't news. . . ." (17)

Later, Lienors says that Guinevere suggested that she come to Spiral Castle (45). Lienors suspects that the Queen did so because she wants to get information on the White Lady and on Morgan-Morgause, whom she associates with the waste lands (45). The White Lady would simply be considered a witch in France (56), and accusations of being on the side of the White Lady will damage one's reputation at Camelot (88). The White Lady is definitively associated with Gawain's Cauldron by Lienors as she goes on the way to Amesbury (202). Recent Arthurian novels and films, such as the television film *Merlin*, scripted in part by Peter Barnes, have pitted the forces of Christianity and paganism directly against each other, but Mitchison, writing in 1955, uses this more oblique method.

Although the recent collection of essays assembled by Ian Firla and Grevel Lindop tries to revive the idea that Graves's conception of the White Goddess deserves attention for its insight into mythology, Andrew Von Hendy, in his magisterial *The Social Construction of Myth*, makes clear the many shortcoming of the Frazer-Weston-Graves school of myth studies, which continue to have such a wide public following through such films as John Boorman's *Excalibur*.

Von Hendy writes:

> . . . Graves belongs to the livelier branch of the [Divine Kingship school] represented by the writings of Jessie Weston and Margaret Murray. Like them, he extrapolates from the assumptions of Frazer and Harrison the disguised survival throughout Christian Europe and into the present of a pagan fertility religion that celebrates a supreme mother-goddess. (194)

Von Hendy at this point in his book has already severely criticized Frazer (92-97) for his inept comparative method by which he came up with an "ahistorical *purée*, not only of social and historical contexts but of literary and dramatic genres and of the talents, motives, and degree of reliability of informants" (93). Indeed, Frazer's approach has long fallen on "general obloquy," as he states (93). Graves, he asserts, created The White Goddess as an "improved, properly generalized *Golden Bough*" (195). The result is "yet another post-romantic, male construction of experience itself as female, and represented as a mysterious woman" (195). Von Hendy bemoans Graves's powerful influence in promoting this idea from "literary fantasy to anthropological verity" (195).

Not only does Mitchison use a Gravesian White Lady in her novel, she keeps Graves contemporary by her creation of an Arthurian world which is contemporary to our own with its heavy reliance on people reading newspapers for information. The flattening out of historical periods through anachronism fits in well with the Frazer-Graves mythology, so depleted of historical specificity and so concerned with grand narrative. A much more historical and sensible study of the Holy Grail is provided by Richard K. Barber in his recent book on the subject. He writes of the tales from the Celtic past, "The problem is that the stories themselves have vanished, leaving only mysterious traces for which the Celtic tellers of tales may not have been ultimately responsible" (11). For Barber, it is better to begin with Chrétien de Troyes, not with comparative mythos, as do the heirs of Frazer. For an insightful speculative account of why the Grail entered literature with Chrétien de Troyes in the late twelfth century, we can turn to Michel Roquebert's *Les Cathares et le Graal*, in which the author posits the Grail as a Catholic response to the challenging Cathar view of the world.

In conclusion, a certain irony today touches upon Mitchison's achievement in *To the Chapel Perilous* since the alternatives that she offers to the Christian school of interpretation of the Grail are attached to the largely dismissed ritual-school view of the Grail offered by Jessie L. Weston and Robert Graves, themselves strongly indebted to the methodologically discredited work of Sir James Frazer. Indeed Mitchison's first chapter centers on the waste land image, which Weston emphasizes in the second chapter of *From Ritual to Romance*. Although the Celtic view of the origin of the Grail has strong adherents today, Mitchison exceeds its usual bounds by connecting the Cauldron of Ceridwen to Robert Graves's eccentric White Goddess theory through her composite figure of Morgan-Morgause. Lienors tells us to accept different patterns of the Grail, but Mitchison does not go far beyond the ritual school of Grail theory to offer any alternatives. We are encouraged to accept the anthropological, ritual-school view of the origins of the Grail rather than develop a truly personal view of it, as the hermit explicitly advocates. The Christian ideas of the origin of the Grail seem to have dated less than the ritual school ideas. Thus, despite the eternal message of tolerance in the novel, *To the Chapel Perilous* is also time-bound by the intellectual currents of the early 20th century.

CARDINAL STRITCH UNIVERSITY

NOTES

[1] For biographies of the much neglected writer Naomi Mitchison, see Benton (1990) and Calder (1997). Benton has no comment to make on *To the Chapel Perilous* other than the unusual evaluation that it may be considered a children's book (142, 188); Calder (213, 217) notes that Mitchison went to Bar Harbour, Maine, in 1953, where her son Avrion was doing cancer research. It was here in a "small and grubby apartment" that she wrote the novel. It was Mitchison's journalist daughter Val (i. e., Valentine), who married a fellow journalist, Marak Arnold-Forster, in London in 1955 (213). Calder remarks that Mitchison was surprised that her daughter was more sympathetic to Christianity than she herself was (214). Calder writes briefly in evaluation of the novel, ". . . . here

Naomi's attempt to fuse together different genres does not quite come off, although there are some splendidly comic vignettes" (217).

[2] Thompson notes that *To the Chapel Perilous* was "the first ironic fantasy of novel length in an exclusively Arthurian setting since Mark Twain's *A Connecticut Yankee in King Arthur's Court* (1985: 152).

[3] The newspaper theme held personal associations for Mitchison, for, as Thompson mentions in his Introduction to the reprint of *To the Chapel Perilous*, Mitchison was a reporter in Austria in 1933, when Chancellor Dolfuss suspended parliament and became dictator. Furthermore, she was later a correspondent for the *Manchester Guardian*, and she also had a daughter and son-in-law who reported for rival newspapers (Thompson 1999: 7-8).

[4] Muriel Whitaker notes that the Grail Castle Corbenic is a place of mystery which is treated inconsistently throughout the *Morte Darthur*. (89).

WORKS CITED

Amey, Michael D. "Constructing a Perilous Chapel: Contesting Power Structures in Naomi Mitchison's *To the Chapel Perilous*," *Arthuriana* 14.3 (Fall 2004): 69-80.

Barber. Richard W. *Holy Grail: Imagination and Belief.* Cambridge: Harvard UP, 2004.

Benton, Jill. *Naomi Mitchison: A Century of Experiment in Life and Letters.* London: Pandora, 1990.

Calder, Jenni. *The Nine Lives of Naomi Mitchison.* London: Virago, 1997.

Firla, Ian, and Grevel Lindop, eds. *Graves and the Goddess: Essays on Robert Graves's* The White Goddess. Selinsgrove, PA: Susquehanna UP, 2003.

Ford, Patrick K. trans. "The Tale of Taliesin." *The Mabinogi and Other Medieval Welsh Tales.* Berkeley: U of California P. 1977.

Graves, Robert. *The White Goddess: A Historical Grammar of Poetic Myth.* Ed. Grevel Lindop. Manchester: Carcanet P, 1997.

Hanks, D. Thomas, Jr. "Malory's Anti-Knights: Balin and Breunys." *The Social and Literary Contexts of Malory's* Morte Darthur." Ed. D. Thomas Hanks, Jr. and associate ed. Jessica Gentry Brogdon. Cambridge: D.S. Brewer: 2000. Pp. 94-110.

Ihle, Sandra Ness. *Malory's Grail Quest: Invention and Adaptation in Medieval Prose Romance.* Madison: U of Wisconsin P, 1983.

Lupack, Alan. Rev. of *To the Chapel Perilous* by Naomi Mitchison; *Arthur, the Bear of Britain* by Edward Frankland; and *Kinsmen of the Grail* by Dorothy James Roberts. *Arthuriana* 11.4 (Winter 2001). Pp. 139-40.

Malory, Thomas. *Works.* Ed. Eugène Vinaver. 2ⁿᵈ ed. Oxford UP, 1971.

Mitchison, Naomi. *To the Chapel Perilous.* London: Allen & Unwin, 1955.

_____. *To the Chapel Perilous.* Introduction by Raymond H. Thompson. Oakland, CA: Green Knight P, 2000.

Nellis, Marilyn K. "Anachronistic Humor in Two Arthurian Romances of Education: *To the Chapel Perilous* and *The Sword in the Stone*." *Studies in Medievalism* 2.4 (1983): 57-77.

Obermeier, Anita. "Postmodernism and the Press in Naomi Mitchison's *To the Chapel Perilous*." *Studies in Medievalism*, forthcoming.

Roquebert, Michel. *Les Cathares et le Graal*. Toulouse: Privat, 1994.

Thompson, Raymond H. "The Grail in Modern Fiction: Sacred Symbol in a Secular Age." *The Grail: A Casebook*. Ed. Dhira B. Mahoney. New York: Garland, 2000. 545-60.

_____. "Interview with Naomi Mitchison. "*Camelot Project Interviews*. Retrieved 15 June 2002. www.lib.rochester.edu/camelot/intrvws/mitchison.htm. 3 pages.

_____. Introduction. *To the Chapel Perilous*, by Naomi Mitchison. Oakland, CA: Green Knight P, 2000. 7-10.

---. *The Return from Avalon: A Study of the Arthurian Legend in Modern Fiction*. Westport, CT: Greenwood P, 1985.

Von Hendy, Andrew. *The Modern Construction of Myth*. Bloomington: Indiana UP, 2002.

Weston, Jessie L. *From Ritual to Romance*. 1920; Rpt. Garden City, NY: Doubleday, 1957.

Whitaker, Muriel. *Arthur's Kingdom of Adventure: The World of Malory's Morte Darthur*. Cambridge: D.S. Brewer/ Barnes & Noble, 1984.

www.ingramcontent.com/pod-product-compliance
Lightning Source LLC
Chambersburg PA
CBHW050412030726
47503CB00006B/2149